The Business Secret Power

LUN SAGE

Copyright © 2019 Lun Sage

All rights reserved.

ISBN: ISBN: 9781073827695

DEDICATION

To God Almighty.

CONTENTS

FOREWORD	1
PRE LESSON: The Purpose Driven Business Exploits	3
LESSON ONE: Quest for Business	15
LESSON TWO: The Inevitable Business Partner	27
LESSON THREE: Be the Creative Boss!	39
LESSON FOUR: Keys to Managing Profit and Loss	49
LESSON FIVE: Understand Business Management Decisions	59
LESSON SIX: Apply Financial Wisdom	69
LESSON SEVEN: The Vital Pros and the Stench Cons	77
LESSON EIGHT: Investment is Key	87
LESSON NINE: Explore The Sense Realm	93
LESSON TEN: Make Teamwork a Habit	99
LESSON ELEVEN: Your Mentality Matters	107
LESSON TWELVE: The Relevance of Money	117
LESSON THIRTEEN: Good Assets Management Techniques	125
LESSON FOURTEEN: Business Longevity has Divine Principles	133
LESSON FIFTEEN: Business Success brings Responsibilities	141
LESSON SIXTEEN: Thought Pattern and Mind Platform	147
LESSON SEVENTEEN: Maximize Your Idea	156
LESSON EIGHTEEN: The Willpower Strategy	177

ACKNOWLEDGMENTS

On the various rungs of life's ladder, I came in contact with individuals who helped to push me up; this is an undeniable fact which calls for appreciation. I am immensely grateful to all. To Barr. Johnson Oshoma and Peter Uwalaka, I appreciate your worthy influence. Big thanks to all my friends, teachers, colleagues and all who contributed positively to making this book a reality.

I owe an eternal gratitude to Madu Abba O, Sam Abah and Martins C.O for showing me great love. Not forgetting great authors whose wealth of inspiration l absorbed immeasurably: Dr David Oyedepo, Myles Munroe, Robert Kiyosaki, John Maxwell, Dr Ben Carson, Robert Schuller, Sam Adeyemi, John Mason, Brian Tracy... Thanks for the privilege to stand on your shoulders. So profound is the impact of Full Gospel Business Men's Fellowship International and Winners' Family worldwide. It has been great experience with you.

FOREWORD

This book is a creative work expressed with unique intelligence. The author presents an irresistible meal -an eye-opener for business creation.

The Business Secret Power teaches business creation insights capable of generating lasting career. It is written by the author to give an expose into the importance of value oriented ideas for a successful business creation. It offers a pragmatic approach to making business yield to us at all times through the application of the amazing creative ideas and techniques exposed in it. It informs, teaches, empowers and gives thorough practical guides to building business by creating value first.

It is written with unique pattern and implored human characters for easy understanding of the insights. It is delineated into twenty-one unforgettable lessons and has the elements required to turn a slow and moribund business to a productive and profitable one. The concepts and terminologies used are well suitable both in business and all career creations. He explored the scripture and ideas from great authors and experienced professionals to clarify the lessons.

The author is an Economist whose wealth of experience as a Banker, Senior Financial Planner (Insurance), Christian Leader and Resource Person are laudable. Here, he used first person narration... Hence, positioned himself as an inspiring business manager and allowed the students and readers to learn in more intimate contact. This technique is unmistakable, inexplicable, highly professional and result-oriented. It could rightly be said that the author diagnosed business secrets and successfully interlocked them with divine principles for unbeatable business creation. He thus, presented a unique business production life cycle without a decline stage. This he made possible by introducing a divine factor, which could offset the decline stage - the peak of creative masterpiece.

This book is indeed unveiling business secrets capable of making you outstanding in your career. You have in your hands a masterpiece for business creation. I therefore recommend this book to all and sundry who wants to live above average. It is a must read for individuals, homes, schools and churches. In deed, it is a training manual for entrepreneurs.

Dr Tina Nweze (JP

Senior Lecturer (EBSU)

PRE-LESSON

This preliminary lesson is an introduction to the creative book you are about to encounter. It teaches how resourceful idea births business creation and influences high networth. It posits the supreme relevance of idea when nurtured with value placement as not mere necessary condition but foundational in career and business creations. A good emphasis on the unlimited power of the mind to attain destiny. This truth was sagely conveyed in explicit cognitive approach without undermining the inevitable partners of business success.

Every business empire, creative invention or career exploit is generated with an invaluable resource known as idea. It is the secret power in this resource that career persons and entrepreneurs depend on to achieve set goals.

This masterpiece digs the depths, searches the bounds and reaches the horizons to teach the right attitudes, strategies and synergies upon which idea when laced on value yield optimally.

This pre lesson unveils three dimensions to purpose

driven business to reset your mind to learn twenty one resourceful lessons for greater efficiency, productivity and profitability in your business.

The Purpose Driven Business

This seminar part was included to the introductory part of this book because of its pivotal role of repositioning the mind for greater impact through its insight. Indeed, testimonies have been tremendous; it is affirmed to generate the creative insight that transmutes to real effects. It also sensitizes both the conscious and the subconscious minds to receive the desired attraction for exploits.

The quest for clarification on an emphatic salient statement during a slide presentation led to the unforgettable lessons in this book. Amazingly, some of the great testimonies from readers have reference to this seminar part. I also had an award of excellence after the maiden power point presentation in a Youth Forum. Certainly, the three dimensions of a purpose driven business have resourceful insights for great goals.

Three Dimensions of a Purpose Driven Business

SELF DISCOVERY

Self discovery is realizing your innate potentials and the ability to explore values. It is about who you are and what you want to become in business. This opens your mind to discover your potentials and creative ideas that are essential to business success. You need to understand yourself in order to thrust your energies in the right direction. Quite interesting, God deposited in every one the required talent to excel in one's career but the ability to explore this talent and align it to the divine purpose wins it all.

Why failure in business? Billy Sunday responds, "More men fail through lack of purpose than lack of talent" To David Star Jordon: "The world stands aside to let anyone pass who knows where he is going."

Business success is a decision. It is a choice you make. Frank Tyger adumbrated, " You future depends on many things but mostly on you" To Zig Ziglar: "What you picture in your mind, your mind will go to accomplish, when you change your pictures, you automatically change yourself." Pat Riley advised, "Don't let other people tell you what you want."

Believe in yourself: Understand that you are the custodian of your business success. God has given you all it takes to succeed. Be confident! Think inwards!

Develop Yourself: Read wide, attend seminars, do some research work. You are encouraged to give quality time to mental work and skill acquisition. Knowledge is key!

Have the Right Attitude: Attitude is the key to a sustained progress in every business. Keith Harrel wrote: "Attitude is everything." It is essentially your attitude that can sustain your business optimally. Attitude is who you are, the character you acquired overtime.

HAVE A BIG PICTURE

The second dimension of a purpose driven business is aligned to your thought pattern. Rene Descartes said, "I think therefore I am." The Bible hits it: "As a man thinketh in his heart, so is he." Prov. 23:7. You see, how big you think determines how far you can go in business. Think big; be unlimited in your plan. Enlarge your mind, think the impossible and explore an unbeatable horizon. Toyota Company is able to excel in the automobile industry because of her mission statement: "Good thinking, good product." You need to understand that you can never be greater than what you think in business. Little wonder Napoleon Hill entitled his best selling book, "Think and grow rich." You can only achieve what you think! Yeah!

Be creative: Every invention and great exploit in business are products of creativity. You can't be outstanding in your business if you do the same old thing repeatedly. Think of a new way of doing your business. Think outside the box. Create new values. Explore the horizon!

Set Mind-boggling Targets: Never set easy-to-achieve target in your business. Let your ultimate target look "crazy" You can break it in bits from a lower rung to a higher one. When you achieve a particular target, you go for a higher one. Remember, success is progressive, it doesn't have a full stop. Work Hard and Smart: Whatsoever is your business, work hard to be the best. There is no smooth road to business success. Success is sure when hard work has direction and meets opportunity. That's smart!

Turning Point for Exploits in business

You must be dissatisfied with low level in life for you

to reach the peak of your business. Get this right: there is no mediocre in the success hall of fame. You should strive to be the best. Let your pursuit be unbeatable!

Build Your Idea: Idea is the king-resource, the "big bang" that launches your business to limelight. It is the impulse which drops down in your mind and seeks to inform, suggest, direct or build a new world in your world. It is gentle and noiseless in nature and could come like a drop depositing an eternal resource. Idea is the thriving platform of all business success; I call it a malleable resource because it can be converted to business success.

Business Creation Steps

* Recognize an idea

* Be original in your idea

* Write it down

* Nurse and nurture your idea

* Reshape and develop your idea

* Test your idea

* Advertise your idea

* Sell your idea

Remember, all the world inventions are products of

ideas: the airplane, computer, television, to mention but a few.

Be Diligent: The scripture alerts, " Seest thou a man diligent in his business? He will stand before kings; he will not stand before mean men." Prov. 22:29.

Diligence entails relentless efforts in the right direction. Do your work as if your life depends on it. This is the secret of outstanding business success. Your business is your primary assignment, get hooked to it and target excellence. Success in business is not about what you are doing but how you do what you do.

Are you a student? Your academic success should be your priority. Let it be directed to what you want to be -who you want to become. Determine to be the best in your choice career. All things are possible. Be unlimited in your mind. The best decision is to study a course that is related to your ability (potential). This is the essential step you need to get right.

To the employees out there: I was shocked to understand that in the world business hall of fame, no employee's name was there. Are you shocked too? What...? Are you still there? Wait a minute! It is not wrong to be an employee, but it is evil to limit your mind on God's big picture for you. Huh! What difference will you make? What value will you add? Count your relevance. If your motivation is only salary, then you have no career there. Yeah!

For employers, get it right! There is nothing wrong with starting small, but don't stop there. Explore! Run your business with bold vision. Picture the future of your business... How far do you want to go? Undoubtedly, the higher your insight the bigger the future of your business.

The scripture alerts, " ...write the vision and make it plain upon tables that he may run that readeth it. For the vision is yet for an appointed time, but at the end it shall speak and not lie. Though it tarry, wait for it; because it will surely come, it will not tarry" Hab. 2:2-3.

Every business or career has the potential to be great. However, right inputs are quintessential. Shoot your career aspiration high. Target global limelight. Develop standards that will stand the test of time. Explore your creativity and satisfy your quest. Thumb up to you!

TAKE STEPS TO WIN

Decision prepares your mind but action delivers result. Business success is not a parcel of gift but a proof of deliberate actions. Take bold steps through right business strategies. Nothing works until you make it to work. Nothing moves until force is applied to it. This gives credence to Newton's 1st law of motion: "Every body will continue in its present state of rest or if it is in motion will continue to move on a straight line unless if acted upon by an impressed force". What a great point!

Push for Success in You Business: Tell your discouragements and excuses to wait; you have a mission to accomplish. Don't wait for opportunities to come to you, go after them!

Don't Quit till You Win: Hold on, don't give up! Every business has inherent ups and downs. When you fail in your business, try again! Learn from Abraham Lincoln, Thomas Edison etc. Remember, there is no failure anywhere until you stop trying.

Conquer Odds

Every business has these inherent obstacles. You must apply right strategies to overcome them.

Face Your Fear: Fear is an unpleasant emotion or thought that comes from a perceived mishap in business venture. This comes in different forms:

a) Fear of starting

b) Fear of criticism

c) Fear of anger

d) Fear of failure

e) Fear of size/position f) Fear of the unknown

Fear makes you believe you cant succeed. It has a lot of reasons to prove its point but faith in God is the strategy to overcome it. William Wingglesworth said; "Fear knocked at my door, I sent faith to open it and I discovered that no one was there." You see! Please step out!

Overcome Mediocrity: This is just being average. it says, "Don't be hot, don't be cold; don't be down and never up." A mediocre is a middle man who is comfortable with average position. In pursuit of business success, many are held back by this obstacle but thinking big will be of immense help. W.F. Kumuyi alarms, "I will not settle for low or middle level when God has promised me the peak." Donald Trump said, "My ultimate pain in life is being the second best at anything, I equate it to failure." Think

big, be unlimited.

Subdue Inferiority Complex: This makes you feel you are not good enough or qualified for the best in business. Undoubtedly, inferiority complex and mediocrity hold people in the same web of low self-esteem. Good motivation is needed. Know who God says you are!

Excuse your Excuses: Excuse has reasons, (genuine if you like) to keep people down perpetually. Excuse all your excuses! John Mason strikes, "If you can find an excuse, don't use it. Most failures are experts in making excuses." Excuses may come in terms of finance, manpower, disability, family background, stature etc, but the advise is: don't use it, determine to succeed in your business. You should remember, "The most unprofitable item ever produced is an excuse." Be smart! Don't buy it! Lighten up your business with positive will power. No excuses!

Questions to Reset your Mind

1). How committed are you to your business?

2). Do you work only for money or also to develop yourself?

3). Have you identified possible obstacles to your

business success? If yes, how do you intend to handle them?

4). How much sacrifice are you willing to make to achieve success in your business?

5). When you fail repeatedly in your business, what do you do?

6). How big is your business dream?

7). Are you waiting for money to start your dream business? Wait no more. You have the answer here. Yeah! You can start business without money.

This is the great insight you have been waiting for. You can now connect...

LESSON 1

QUEST FOR BUSINESS

Three persons approached me after my career talk on the Three Dimensions of Purpose Driven Business Exploits principally to understand my insightful statement, "You can start business without money".

"Is it possible?" Somebody asked. "Can it really work?" Another doubted. "How? Tell me you don't mean what you said" Was yet another question. The last person was more curious than others. But one thing was common, all wanted to know the reality of what I said. Let me make it clear here.

Starting Business Without Money

This may sound like a bombshell. Yeah! That is the undeniable truth you are about to discover. Get ready to explore the unlimited secret power in you.

We are about to start a business creation journey, this

book will take us to the core target of career persons and entrepreneurs.

Business is an enterprise which involves people playing different roles in establishing and developing goods and services for the satisfaction of the consumers. Business involves both tangible and intangible wealth creation. It is multi-dimensional in scope...

More than this, a lot of things are involved in business. This book is not only going to be practical but also critically analytical where necessary. All hanging questions would be locating right answers as we delve into the crux of this book. Get ready to hit it big! Remember, the target of every successful business is value creation and consumer satisfaction.

"Let us discuss this topic later", I told them. That was because I needed a conducive place and more time for explanations. I also knew that it may be difficult to give convincing explanations without good illustrations. Yes, I needed some aids: the first two that came to my mind were writing board and a marker pen. It means I would be the teacher while they would be the students.

Two of the prospective students were important members of the society. But each had failed in various businesses at different times; the third person was yet to start a business. Their enthusiasm were the same and that was what assured me that it would make a good class. They would be ready to learn...

When I suggested changing the explanation of my puzzling statement to another day their response was like a chorus, "Why? We want it now !", they said.

It took quite a couple of minutes to break through their curiosity. It's all for a better understanding and explanation. At last we agreed on a date, venue and time.

When I returned home that day, different thoughts flickered through my mind. The spirit in me whispered something, "This is picking an infinite career". I could not question the spirit because I have had several dreams which pointed to the same fact. But was that what I really wanted? Yeah, I reasoned: I have identified need, it's time to create value... Again, two great insights crept in: Habakkuk 2:2-3 and Robert Kiyosaki's inspiration: "The best way to learn is to teach what you want to learn and the best way to be rich is to help others become rich."

I knew I have had the opportunity of impacting lives with life changing wisdom that would build their careers. Should it just be like what I used to teach? I pondered. Alone in the room, I tried to think . Think... Yes, plan... And... Is it going to be something different?

"Teach them how to create business starting with the infinite resource (idea)." That was the instruction from a still voice. Quickly, I started a cursory plan, but later changed it to a thorough (completely detailed) plan. The mastermind beckoning...

When we met on Saturday at exactly 10 am, I gave them the excerpt of my plan, I addressed them in a totally different way and made them to understand that we were really into something serious.

During my introduction, I said: "These lessons are centered on business creation. They are aimed at empowering the mind to start the business empire with an idea and transmute it to reality. This course will last twenty-one weeks. You are expected to have a full understanding of the secrets power of idea in business creation. Each week is going to be a new topic and some hours for strategy, research and development.

Saturdays would be lecture days. To my surprise,

the three persons were still eager to go through this "School". Yes, I call it school because my spirit told me it was going to be more than what I was seeing...

I gave them the teaching outline and we started that day with the first lesson "Quest for Business"

I observed how their eyes dilated in anxiety

immediately I wrote the topic on the board with capital letters. As I wrote on the board, I remembered my teaching strategy: teaching with illustrations, asking questions and answering questions.

It was just the right time for me to know the names of the students. Matt and Jeff were important members of the society, both had held political positions and had also failed in other businesses at various times.

Nic was a prospective businessman. He seemed to be much hit by fear of business failure that he never started. I encouraged them to jot notable points and always gave them time to do so.

Nic asked his first question. "How much will you charge us per week or for the period of twenty-one.

I knew such question would come. It was just normal to expect it, I also knew why Nic asked the question. His countenance told me. Matt and Jeff stared at Nic, I could also read their impressions.

Their mind set was totally different from Nic's. They were ready to pay any amount, what they wanted was result.

"Don't worry about the fee, let's hit our target first", I replied him. "Hit target first?". Nic stammered disbelievingly. That was the reply he least expected.

I answered "Yes" again, now with a smile. I tried to be more lively and radiated a feasible smile. I knew exactly what I was doing, but Nic did not. I was already applying what I wanted to teach. Yes, starting a business without money. Moreover, I was testing something; something that is capable of generating more money than the money Nic was talking about. It is about the business of making a career of great reward.

Wow! It was quite amazing, learning how to start business without money. Ideas tickling...

I said something remarkable and I saw it sink deep into the students. "At the end of this course you should be able to discover yourself and how to apply your energies to generate business capable of making you great and fulfilled even at an old age."

Nic flickered his head, it was as if he was struck by something. "Is it possible?" He asked.

"Yes !" I answered him. I decided not to go in details because he would be more confused... But I saw each of them note the statement.

After an overview of the topic. I unveiled the first secret of career and business creation.

Secret No. 1

Plan big but start small

The future belongs to those who dream big dreams but start small. Bob Gass advised, "Start with something small". You should know that growth is what determines the viability of any business. If you start small, you will be quick to understand the movement of the business; management will be easier until you are able to control it at a bigger level.

How Can I Start Business Without Money?

This was exactly my next point but Jeff seemed to be running out of patience. He asked this question with great expectation.

"Listen very well", I told the students. You do not start business with money, but first by taking the following steps:

1. Identify Opportunities and Needs

This is an important step to starting a business. Any business founded on the needs of the people and identified opportunities can't be short of success. If you must

hit it big, it must be by identifying opportunities and

the needs of people. Create value first!

2. Initiate a Business with your Idea

An idea is the king resource in generating business exploits. Think, having

identified an opportunity or need; use your idea to initiate the business. "Idea rules the world"- Sam Adeyemi. Success is an offspring of idea, idea born of deep thoughts. Think well! Idea comes like an impulse, identify it, write it, use it! (Detail on lesson seventeen).

3. Understand Your Potentials:

Ideas are symbolic pictures of potentials.

Business yield maximum result if rooted on potentials. Undertake a business that you are endowed with the requisite potential. Your ability determines the height of your business success.

Think! Is your potential in line with your prospective business? The answer

should be yes, if you want maximum result.

4. Have a Business Plan: This is the blue-print of how you want you business to be. It should include both the target and the strategies to be applied in the business.

Business is directionless without a plan.

Imagine a business without a plan, it can only exist in theory. The importance of a business plan was highlighted by Maurice Witzer when he said, "You seldom get what you want unless you plan for it".

Do more than having a business idea, identifying opportunities or thinking about your rich potential; you must plan your business if you want growth and stability.

5. Consider Business Environment: Locating and carrying out a business in an environment is profitable when the environment does not work against the business. Is the environment conducive for your prospective business? What extra work do you have to do?

6. Search for information: Business works with information. Be ready to scan for information that will be relevant to your prospective business.

7. Make a demand forecast: What is the demand likely to be? Think about some strategies you will adopt to increase the demand. You should be able to fore-cast the future demand and plan for it. Make adequate preparation for management supply too. .

All these points mentioned above could be regarded as

business plan or survey. They are the elements that initiate business operation.

I wrote these points down on the board and allowed the students to write them down on their notes.

When their attention was at it's peak, I had no doubt within my mind that the first lesson had begun smoothly, but I needed to hit it closer to dissolve all hanging confusion. "You don't need money to start business. What you need is to plan first with yourself, have an idea, plan with it," I told them raising my voice a bit.

Quite interesting! I noticed Matt and Jeff nod satisfactorily, while Nic looked intently at my eye- balls. I continued, "If you start business with money, it is bound to fail."

Immediately I made this statement I discovered that Matt was some what unconformable. Something was rattling in his mind I observed. I observed him keenly with the corner of my left eye.

"Excuse me sir !", Matt said raising his right forefinger. I should allow him to ask his question. "Yes , Matt !", I said.

"How can we start business without money?". I smiled with unmistakable radiance, walking closer to the students. Just to answer the question, Nic mused "I know the answer !".

Interesting! My heart bulged with happiness. At least somebody wanted to attempt the question. I should allow Nic.

"We are told not to start business with money, but by first identifying opportunities, and applying our potentials /ideas in a well laid business plan. I think money can come later".

I stared at Nic as he answered the question. Quite interesting! I was impressed particularly on his last statement, "I think money can come latter."

Yes, money is important in business, but it is not the starting point; it can come latter.

The success of your business depends on it's starting point. Yes, without money. How you start a business gives you more than 50% success. This means that you must have achieved more than fifty percent success in business just by satisfying the elements enumerated above. Many people who wait for money to start business always ended as business failures because money is not the beginning. You can enquire from the two very important members of the society - Matt and Jeff. Yeah!

Matt started his business with $15,000 while Jeff started with $10,000. Both failed because they had much money to start with but didn't have the grand plan (business plan). Money is not the foundation of a business, it only completes the business operational requirements. A house with good foundation can never sink, so is a business with the right foundation- foundation built on good plans (not money).

"I will go through your work in our next meeting", I told them. The first lesson had ended well. As a foot-note, I gave them the second secret of business creation.

Secret No. 2

Don't start business with money, but with yourself

(your idea). Think of value placement in the society.

LESSON 2

THE INEVITABLE BUSINESS PARTNER

I determined to hit it big together with the students. I also researched and developed my business plan. It was all about starting business without money. Idea is indeed supreme when laced on value, yet money is an inevitable partner.

I delineated the twenty-one lessons on business creation aimed at making a successful career into twenty-one weeks. There would be three weeks lessons making a semester and two semesters making a session (that is an academic year of six weeks) in the business creation school.

It would take four academic years (three and half sessions) covering twenty-one weeks and twenty- one lessons to complete this school. Exams would be taken at the end of each semester to test the understanding of the students in the theoretical and practical works.

The plan was comprehensive but I still made room for

improvements. My mind told me that something bigger than my plan was on the way. It flashed back to the first instruction. The mastermind!

I was to teach the second lesson on 10th August. It was a bright day in deed. I must not forget the time (10 am).

I took time to prepare for the second lesson hoping to have another successful day. Gush! An unusual joy sizzled down my heart; I couldn't really tell, I began to give God thanks. Thanks and thanks and... I felt like not stopping; but I should not disappoint the students. I must go, it was almost time.

I was just at the lecture venue two minutes before the time. "Yes, I must show example by good time management", I muttered within my mind.

When I entered inside, I discovered that the students had come quite earlier than the scheduled time. Not only that, there was another shock. There were six other students. Each of the students came with two of his friends.

Wow! Nine students in all. It was becoming more interesting! "What should I do?" My brain reverberated looking for a quick solution.

One thing was obvious, I was not going to repeat the

first lesson and on the other hand I wasn't going to start the second lesson with the new students; if I do, they would miss the foundation of business creation principles. This also means that they would loose more than fifty percent in their prospective businesses.

I should think of a way of carrying everybody along and ensuring their maximum understanding of the lessons - I looked at my schedule again; Saturday for my new teaching class and Sunday for Church service. The remaining five days have been occupied. But ...

"This is an infinite career, why not use the remaining five days for the classes, it could be an inestimable resources to be invested in the business." The still voice crept in, talking slowly but convincingly.

I remembered the topic I was to teach that day "The inevitable business partner". I was about to teach them how to use money to run business. But it was my own turn to use my own money to run my own business. It's all about practical work...

I addressed the new students in a couple of minutes and assured them they would be able to create an invaluable career at the end of the course. For us to achieve this target, I must start with the first lesson but because I have some students that I would be taking on the second lesson, they should have their own class on Monday August 12.

An idea struck me which 1 later made a culture in the Business Creation School. I handed to the new students copies of my seminar work, the pre lesson note- The three dimensions of a purpose driven business to study, in order to reset their minds and inspire them for the main lessons.

It was a good development. To the new students, the schedule was okay. But before they left, I registered their names: Mano, Dan, Chizo, Kellen, Mike and Lekky.

They were looking keen and ready for business. I could bet they would do better than the first three students.

I demanded from the old students their plans and research work on the last topic. "Quest for Business" laying emphasis on the vital statement, "You can start business without money" Each of the students had well detailed business plan; their powerful ideas when combined with potentials and if complimented by the inevitable partner would make them great entrepreneurs.

Jeff looked scientific in his proposed business plan. He

could be a "Thomas Jefferson"

"You all have good business plans. This is the beginning of the business. You have more than fifty percent success already even without introducing money", I encouraged them . I then meandered to the day's lesson, "The inevitable Business Partner".

Now that you have climbed the first rung of the ladder of creating business through resourceful idea. You are going to take a step higher by introducing money into your business.

Secret No. 3

Money doesn't start a business but it plays a vital and indispensable role in business.

Robert Kiyosaki said, "If you want more money simply change your thinking". Quoting him further, "Education and Wisdom about money are important. Start early, buy books, go to seminars; practice... start small".

Fred Siegel asserted, "There are no magic paths to riches. You are going to have to work hard until your money start to work for you". You have to understand money and it's role in your business. There are laws which guide money. You must adhere to these laws.

Before I stated the laws of money I gave them the fourth secret of business creation.

Secret No. 4

Don't embark on a new business with all your money, apply wisdom. Develop your idea, plan!

You must be sensitive to business investment decisions. There is no financial wisdom putting all your money in a business especially at the early stage. Get acquainted with the business before introducing more money. You must apply financial wisdom to maximize profit.

OBEY THE LAWS OF MONEY

Immediately I wrote this on the board, apt attention was the expression written all over the face of the students. Their reactions were close to surprise. I keenly observed the expression on their faces. I was sure somebody would ask a question .

It was Matt, his question depicted his low level of understanding about money and his past mistakes.

"Do you mean there are laws that guide money?" Matt asked.

This question revealed to me that some of the students were about discovering another point where they got it wrong. "Yes, there are laws which guide money if you want it to be productive." I answered.

We are going to study these laws, the practical work will show us how they work. The laws of money start as well as finish the role of money in ensuring business profitability.

1. Care for money: This is the first law. You have to care for money by protecting it

justlike a mother would do unto her child. Do not be harsh, rough or careless with it. The way you handle it determines whether it will stay or go. Many business men lost financial dignity in their business as soon as money wasintroduced because they were careless with money. Care for money, nurse it like a baby. This is the first step to be financially savvy.

2. Save money: Money saved is better than money earned. It is not how much you make in business but how much you can save. If you make $1000 in business daily and spend all; your business would soon liquidate. Look at another person who makes $500 and save

$200. It is not the amount you make, it is the amount you save. If you aim at profitability and growth in business, you must save part of your earnings.

If you aim at making a successful career, you should save at least 10% of your earnings. "10% is too small, I can save 50%", Nic thundered. "Yes, 10%. You have other expenses to make. You must pay your staff and buy materials and equipment. You will learn about this later", I responded.

I wanted the students to understand me clearly. I should not go into details on payment system in business because they have not gotten to that stage yet.

Quickly, I moved to the third law of money.

3. Invest money: Money saved sometimes never yielded anything without investment. Money invested is better than money saved, because it has the potential to increase or multiply.

The ultimate way of making money generate high business growth is to invest it in the acquisition of high yielding assets. For a short-term investment, you can use it for fast business turn-over.

You can only re-coup business benefits through investment. You must invest wisely!

I should always make my explanation brief for easy

understanding and assimilation of the students. At this point I thought it wise to give them the fifth secret of business creation.

Secret No. 5

*Care for money, save, invest and monitor your investments

This secret is important, it is not as simple as you think but forms the heart of business creation.

When the students finished writing, I made a statement targeted at preparing their minds towards an important point they should understand during the course period. It was about money and business. "Money is important in business", I told them. You must work hard, but more than that , working hard to make money only doesn't put one in the place of business creation which is our target. Remember, our aim is to have a successful business of high net worth and influence.

Listen, don't work only for money, but you should be able to attain the level where money should work for you. I was beginning to predict the students. Immediately I made the last statement, I knew Jeff would ask a question. The way he dilated his eyes also corroborated my instinct.

"Money work for me?" He asked standing and pointing directly at himself. I should hit his question straight. I knew he would understand better when I take them on lesson twelve -The Strength of Money.

There would be a level you get to in business exploit where you don't struggle again to make money. At this stage you have investments capable of duplicating the money invested in such an amazing way. Your staff strength must also have gotten to point where you only have to motivate them to give you the best of what you have envisioned. Here growth and profit are maximum through good management decisions.

Jeff nodded as I explained. I could also see smiles on the faces of Matt and Nic. There was no doubt they understood the point.

In the research and practical work, I encouraged the students to invest $1000 each in their proposed business. But since they are not allowed to start any business in real terms yet until they have studied this manual, they should set the money apart and study the laws of money and the tips on how to make money work for them. Think about money, look for a way to make it profitable. Money is an agent, it is also a messenger, let it run your errands. Be the creative boss!

Take actions that will put your resourceful ideas to global limelight.

LESSON 3

BE THE CREATIVE BOSS

What a real business exploit I knew it would be! I have accepted to create my own business by stirring up the idea in

me. I should not be limited by odds but should focus on making positive impact and becoming a solution to people.

Be the Creative Boss! The third lesson began. Yes, I should be the creative boss through strategic thinking. I must take initiatives, I must think outside the box...

The six (new) students have given me the challenge I needed to handle as the creative boss. There would be six lecture days. I knew why I expanded my plan like that... It is a career worth making one outstanding, I should understand. Without any doubt in my mind; I knew that more students were coming. I decided to make provision for six lecture days according to their batches.

Being a real boss for the first time, I should prove it by

efficiency and not by pride.

I have pushed every thing aside, I must pursue this career. An infinite career capable of making me fulfilled . My thirst for creativity.

On Monday August 12, the second batch of the students gathered at the lecture venue. I wasn't surprised when I saw their number - eleven students. I had planned and made provision for them (the additional five students).

Quickly, I addressed them with perfect courtesy - making them feel important. I registered their names and asked them to come for their lecture the following day (Tuesday13). I could see smiles on their faces as they left the class. Moreover, l handed the Pre lesson note to them to study as has become the culture...

I started lesson one with the second batch, "Quest for business" Not forgetting my emphasis on, "You can start business without money". Really, my expectation was not cut short. There were all brilliant students. Though at first some of them thought it was completely incredible to start business without money, but they all left with their minds convinced beyond reasonable doubt that money doesn't start business.

The third lecture with the first batch was splendid. It started at exactly 10 am. It was all about being the boss. The boss must be a good time manager because business could be a total failure if time is not well managed. "Time is business", they say.

When I introduced the third lesson. It was really great - mind boggling!

"Be the creative boss !" I could see laughter cross the face of the students. "Yes, I am the creative boss". Matt thundered "Me too!" Jeff adumbrated . There was a feast of laughter in the class. I wasn't exempted. For a minute, I allowed the laughter to rock ... Yes, I knew it was also part of the learning technique. They should express themselves positively.

Straight to Business!

I started without further delay. You should not dream to be a permanent staff in somebody's business but aim at being the boss of your own business. The creative boss creates his world.

Don't forget our target is to make global impact in business creation. This could be a sure reality if you can be the creative boss.

You are now the boss! I looked at the students, there

were smiles of good self-esteem across their faces. Yes they are…

YOUR BUSINESS AND YOU

a. The owner (boss): The boss is different from the business. Your business should be separate from you. It should be a separate entity. You should be there as a co-ordinator who deserve his own reward.

b. Family Members: Just as your business is separate from you; it is also separate from your family. That means, your family members should depend on your salary or wages, not on the entire business proceeds.

"What !" Jeff shouted. I knew this point hit him hard but that's the essence of the lesson. It should break to build. I was creating an entirely new mind set in them. The harvest would be great!

YOUR BUSINESS AND OTHERS

a. Staff: Your staf fare the engine room behind your business success. If you empower them they will increase your business efficiency

.Handle them with care and caution, their welfare should be considered along side with profitability.

b. Customers/Clients: There is nothing like business without the demand of products or services.

Customers/clients are the consumers of your business products or services. They are the priority. Please treat them with care and respect. You are not superior to your customers/clients because without them your business is completely void.

c. Your environment: Things and people around you form your business environment. They largely contribute to the success or otherwise of your business Be environmental friendly. Take good care of your environment and treat your neighbours as important as you would want them treat you.

The success of your business does not depend on what you don't see, it rather depends on what you see (your environment).

KEEP ACCOUNT

You are the boss! Please keep proper account of all the inflows and outflows of your business. You should be able to initiate and monitor an accounting process capable of accounting for all the incomes and expenditures of your business.

Monitor your business undertakings and teach your staff the importance of accounting and accountability. Remember, it is business not a fun- fare.

KNOW YOUR BUSINESS PRODUCTIVITY

You should know your business productivity and your staff strength per time or at various point in time. This could go a long way in determining how to push the productivity of your business higher or to find the best way to handle an impending decline.

You should keep your eyes down in your business. This is what makes you the boss. Prove your status by work! As your business increases, assign roles to various staff or managers, but make sure you oversee their activities. When the students finished writing, I thought it wise not to leave them with only principles but to strike them harder by highlighting some secrets of wealth creation.

Secret No. 6

* Have a dream to be the boss of your own business not a permanent staff of another person's business.

Think of becoming the boss, this is the sure way of making your business success a reality.

Secret No. 7

Understand that your business is a separate entity. It must be separated from you and your family. Don't suffocate it!

ACTION PACK!

* Don't be held by the past, think of the future - that is the place of your business exploits. Aim at creating business capable of improving yourself worth, net worth and influence.

* Don't limit your business growth, make provision for improvement. As you plan your business growth, make room for new ideas.

* Start small but aim high: this is the sure way to hit your goal. It is not bad to start small, but it is

unacceptable to remain small in business.

I just remembered that I was teaching them the third lesson. Yes, three lessons mark a semester. They should be tested to ascertain the level of their understanding. The exam would qualify them to go for the next three lessons (second semester).

I took time to explain to the students the importance of the exam to their careers and their business creation. You must pass both the theory questions and the research and practical before you learn the next lessons.

I could read the enthusiasm on the faces of the students. I was also enthusiastic because I would be testing my own business.

"I will beat all of you", Nic mused. "Says who?", Jeff adumbrated. "Me; of course", Nic retorted looking unperturbed. "What... I'm sure I'll be the best", Matt opposed.

Talking to the students; I said, "No need to be in a hurry to talk, next Saturday would prove it". I scheduled the exam by 8 am. It was going to be an hour exam. They would take an hour recess waiting for the result before they take the next lesson if they qualified.

On Monday August 19, I taught the second batch the

second lesson. I discovered that three students in the second batch were doing excellently well. Though all of them were brilliant students, Dan, Chizo and Mike were quite outstanding, not even Matt, Jeff and Nic could beat them, I was sure.

I was convinced these students would turn the society to a better place after their studies in the Business School.

This thought created a new joy in me. I could feel this joy erupt from my heart. It rose like an impulse steadily moving up until it lubricated my face with a seasoned smile.

"Thank you Lord!" I said. I also remembered what happened when I took the third batch on the first lesson, there was an unimaginable thirst to acquire the knowledge of business creation. There were also six new students that day. I registered the students and scheduled their lecture days to be Wednesdays.

On Wednesday, there were seven more students, I registered them and scheduled their lectures on Thursdays before taking the fourth batch on their first lesson.

The fifth batch (Thursday students) gave me the biggest surprise of all. They came with thirteen new students, among them were four female students Julie,

Suz, Flora and Jessy. When I was registering them, I solicited their understanding and cooperation by announcing that their lecture would be on Fridays. Also, there won't be registration of new students until after twenty four weeks (the end of an academic year) in Business School.

I knew I was the only teacher, the manager and owner of the business. I should expand my plan to hit my target. Yes, I must be unlimited by delineated into six batches of 3, 6, 5, 6, 7, 13 taking improvement!

Thank you Lord! I now have forty students and their lectures once a week (a day for each batch) except Sundays.

Most of these students were graduates from different high institutions, others were politicians and business men/ women. Some wanted to correct the mistakes of their business failures, others wanted to start it fine... The journey to business creation is practical.

LESSON 4

MANAGING PROFIT AND LOSS IN BUSINESS

I have resolved to take up this new career (my business) where my potential and passion lie. In my reflection I pondered, "Am I making profit or incurring loss?" This thought hung on my mind as I was preparing to take the fourth lecture that morning. Profit? Yes, profit! Was it the right time to think about profit? I paused to think. But definitely not incurring a loss. Break-even was another word which struck my mind. Break-even?

It was a peaceful morning, the weather was calm and cool. Two prime things were on my mind - the exam and marking the beginning of a new semester by teaching the students a very important topic in business creation "Managing profit and loss in business".

The students came quite on time, I could see readiness on their faces. What happened that morning made me to remember my school years when students always say that smoke was coming out of one's head on the eve or the day of an exam. But such smoke seems to be invisible because I never saw it physically

.At exactly 8am the exam started. I was careful in setting their questions; the questions were targeted at testing the depth of their understanding in both the theories and the research and practical works. The three lessons were also equally represented..

I knew their success would mark a giant step to their dream business exploits, and my dream. Yes, my dream!

Success! This was just the summary of the outcome of the exam. I was so elated so were the students.

Did Nic keep to his promise? Quite great! He did. There were some remarkable things in their results. Matt and Jeff performed better in the theories than the research and practical works. Nic was as good in the research and practical works as he was in the theories.

To Matt and Jeff I thought of a way to turn them to be more pragmatic in the research and practical aspects of their business.

Nic needed to overcome the fear of starting and fear of failure. He had a depot of excellent business acumen unutilized.

After addressing the two groups, I encouraged Nic to read my book entitled, "The Success Within". I was sure it would be the right inspiration to his challenge. He must overcome fear and take a bold step.

We resumed the second semester that morning with smiles on our faces. "Yes, it is working!" I said within my mind.

MANAGING PROFIT AND LOSS IN BUSINESS

This lesson was targeted at making the prime aim of business realizable.

Making profit

Growth in business lies primarily on the ability to make profit. Hence, profit is essential for business continuity. Think of engaging in business capable of generating profit, but never target profit at the expense of quality products or services. Let your high profit come as through your excellent quality products or services.

Jeff seem not to completely agree with my explanation. His question portrayed that. "But Inferior products sometimes sell faster than quality products. How can we maximize sales to make big profit?".

Huh! Is this you? As Jeff was asking his question, smile crossed my fat check. How I wish I could hide it but... I knew what Jeff meant by his question. That was the simple reason behind people's one minute success and another minute business failure (they lay poor business foundation by producing fake or inferior goods).

Sales may be maximized with inferior goods or services to generate high profit for just a short time. This short time profit cannot make stable business growth. It frustrates business dream when you hook to your ultimate target. It falls back like a boomerang and crushes the business destiny.

Huh, are you still there? You better change your mind. Yes, think again if your target is creating business capable of making you fulfilled. No need to talk much on this, you can ask Matt and Jeff.

Secret No.8

Match profitability with quality products or services. Never think of providing low quality services or inferior goods in order to maximize profit, it brings failure in business at the long run.

It will only leave you at a mediocre level -a "comfortable failure" status. Give the best; you will reap the best!

Loss at the beginning of a business...

"Oh, that ends the business!", I heard Nic say in a low voice. That was no surprise; this is a school. We learn the right decisions and actions to replace our past mistakes. It is all about learning and the application of the knowledge acquired. The aim of a business venture is to make profit; breaking-even is never the resting place and incurring a consistent loss should be avoided.

Make profit... Hit it big! But some time business may not begin this way. Loss may occur at the start of a business.

The question is, "How do we manage loss at the beginning of a business?". There is no need to panic when there is loss at the beginning of a business venture. What you need is to be diligent with the business decisions: inflows and outflows. You should be able to understand through a feasibility analysis, the time-lag you need to cross from loss to break-even and subsequently maximize profit.

The loss at the beginning of a business may only be investment reaction. This implies the action of business investment before it is due to recoup benefits.

Understand that some business takes short time while others take long time (long run) before benefits could be recouped. Hence, loss may be unavoidable at the beginning of such business. You also need to understand that there are forces which regulate business operation . These forces undoubtedly determine the business life.

As I explained, the students listened with apt attention, but not when I talked about "forces". "What forces ?", Matt asked looking a bit lost. I recognized the fact that I was teaching them the secrets and principles of business creation so this knot must be untied at least for the benefit of Matt and ...

UNDERSTANDING MARKET FORCES

Demand and supply are the controlling forces of all business undertakings. You must understand how they affect your own business.

The former is about the quantity a consumer (buyer) is ready and willing to buy at a particular price, time and place. While the later is the quantity the producer (seller) is ready and willing to sell at a particular time, price and place. What makes these two forces important is that they determine the position of your business -profit or loss.

Whether goods or services, the inter-play of these two forces will place you at your position (success or failure). Think about business, think about demand and supply. You must know how they affect your business.

I went on to explain to the students that although these forces can control business naturally, they could also be controlled or regulated by a business man to maximize profit. You need to know this and apply the knowledge now.

That was indeed a good one. I saw Nic nod satisfactorily. There were yet few other points I noted which I had not mentioned. It was just the right time to mention them I remembered; though as important as they were, I didn't go in details because I had already unveiled them when I thought laws of money.

There are three important things that will make you what you want to be in business - (a) make profit (b) save profit (c) invest profit.

Your business acumen is tests positive when you are able to make profit. It doesn't however end there, you must be able to save and invest. This process generates business growth. It doesn't stop here .

"Where does it stop, then?", Jeff mused, almost half-mindedly.

"That is why you need to go through the whole lessons with diligence. Generating business ought not to have an end until you are able to create a business empire capable of making maximum profit in an auto-

state.

I was laconic in my answer but believed it was satisfactory. Jeff also affirmed so. What do you say?

Spending Expected Profit

Through my research; I should tell the students what had crashed promising businesses of many business men. Most business failures were the result of spending envisaged business profits. When profit looks certain and imminent, don't spend part of your capital with the hope that you would make enough profit to replace part of the capital used and boost your business. This is a mistake as sure as death in killing a business.

The truth is that expected profit is never a profit until it comes; it may however not come as you think. Even when it comes, it is for the business growth (be wise!).

No matter how diligent you were, you would discover your financial decision errors when the profit comes.

It was like something pinched Matt by his left side, the way he bent sharply told me. I had paused to know what it was only to hear him scream, "That is correct Sir!" At this point I proceeded to state the ninth and tenth secret of business creation.

Secret No. 9

Understand how the forces of demand and supply affect your business. You can explore them positively to maximize profit.

Secret No. 10

Don't spend expected profit before it arrives. It is the greatest error and killer of business.

Little wonder it was, I have started thinking differently, my horizon was gradually increasing... I can see it: a transformation of imagination to a business reality. Thinking like the creative boss! My new position became highly demanding more hard work and commitment. That's smart!

I was taking the classes in turns according to their batches. Forty students taught by one person. That's great, but calls for fresh initiative.

LESSON 5

UNDERSTAND BUSINESS MANAGEMENT DECISIONS

Good management decision is just it. Use the present to hit the future! Focusing more on the future using the present, I was planning

how to help the students hit their goals as to hit my own business goal. Creative investment...

I remembered the words of Zig Ziglar, "What you picture in your mind, your mind go to work to accomplish. When you change your pictures, you automatically change yourself." Bertrand Russell said, "Nothing is so exhausting and futile as indecision". To Herbert Porchnow, "There is a time when we must firmly choose the course which we will follow or the relentless drift of events will make the decision for us".

As I ruminated over these words, I could see the hidden truth. Yes, my decision and action could make or mar the chances of meeting my business goal. But one thing was certain I knew; if I must hit my target, the students must first hit theirs. If I could be the solution to their needs, then I must by default have attracted permanent solution to my life challenges or needs. No doubt, this is the core insight in Robert Kiyosaki's inspiration: "The best way to learn is to teach what you want to learn and the best way to be rich is to help others become rich."

I discovered that the students were yet to t understand my purpose. Yes, why I have not demanded for tuition fee. Was I such benevolent to organize these important lectures free? That was a common question on their minds. More than ten students had asked me questions relating to, "Why no fee?" My focus not being on immediate financial reward but on value placement has started generating a flow of solutions leading to financial reward.

I was satisfied with the students enthusiasm and willingness to pay for the lectures. But the fact was that I had something much bigger in mind. I had interviewed the students and was able to discover one important thing. More than half of the number of students don't have money to run their proposed businesses after their training. Most of them don't know how and where to raise money. They would be useful resources in helping me to achieve my goal. They will also achieve their goals by exploring the resources in them. They could apply their secret power to generate other complements to business success...

My new plan had given my business the status of a full-fledged school. It was going to be a school after school". This means, it would be admitting different people with different academic qualifications with the aim of teaching them how to explore the secret power of idea and principles of business creation.

I gave my dream school a definite name: Lun Sage Business School (LSBS).

The plan was comprehensive (completely thorough). The execution of such business plan would need money and other resources like land as well as human resources. My instinct told me it was going to work, and I believed it. I was made to recognize my instinct. It had always led me aright and I was obliged to obey when it instructs. The Still Voice! The mastermind!

It was really an amazing experience – beating my own imagination. "My lines are falling unto me in pleasant places" (Psalm 16:6) was the scriptural verse which flashed my mind. It was just the beginning...

Three students sent three different parcels to me with short notes containing their names and brief comment inside, (in thick brown envelopes).

It was these parcels that made me to understand that some of the students were very important members of the society more than I knew.

Jessy was a Commissioner's wife. Apart from the lump sum of money she gave to me, her note read something very interesting. Her husband was interested in the business school and would like to meet with me in a month's time. Other parcels contained money and words of commendation for a good work.

"It is working!" I said as a fresh aura of joy sizzled down my heart. The students could read the joy on my radiating face as I taught the lesson of the day " Understanding business management decisions" .

Each lesson was targeted at empowering the students in a specific area of business creation. I always tried to be a living application of each lesson.

It was just the right time to teach them management decisions as regards profit, capital and payments.

CAPITAL AND PROFIT IN BUSINESS

The ignorance of some people on basic business concepts contributed to about 20% percent of business failures in different countries of the world. A critical study on the reasons for business failure revealed that many people fail in business daily because they are ignorant of some basic business concepts. The two afore-listed concepts were among the top on the list according to my finding.

As I wrote these two concepts on the board, Nic exclaimed, "Is that not repetition sir?"

"Repetition?", I retorted with a weak smile. A still voice whispered to my mind, "So we would have had another business failure."

Capital: This is what a business man uses in running his business. It may be fixed or liquid asset injected into a business which has the ability of recouping benefits through wise investment decisions.

Profit: is the benefit recouped from the business. It is a product of wise capital investment decision. Profit is gross earnings minus salaries and other accrued expenses (net profit). Gross profit can simply be defined as income minus expenditure.

The first management wisdom to apply is to be able to differentiate capital from profit. These are two things that must be distinguished. Capital is the mother of profit and profit the product of capital invested.

#Secret No. 11

Don't pay with capital, pay with profit. Your balance will be added to your business to increase your capital base.

As I wrote down this secret, my mind drove round this lesson, I remembered I had missed the guiding secret in management decision.

Secret No. 12

Your business is what you make it; your decision can also place you in your position. If you desire excellence make excellent decisions.

Think of expanding your business by expanding your capital investment. You can add your net profit to realize this task. Learn to be diligent in profit management to avoid loss, even when profit is possible. Jeff flickered his head and asked, "Is it possible to incur a loss when profit is possible?".

Good question, "Yes!", I responded. Wrong management decision can make expenditure overwhelm income just after observing a possible profit. This happens when one is carried away by the joy of an expected profit. "Spend more!". Is always the demand for mismanagement. If heeded to, the profit is struck out piercing into the capital. What you have before you is great loss leading to business failure.

"Wow!" Jeff screamed. His eyes rolled over and over until they located Matt's and both smiled. The smile was that of 'eureka!' -I have found it!

I looked at the pendulum clock which hung on the left side of the class room block where we used as our lecture venue. The time reminded me something... It pointed at the rungs of a ladder "higher!" Yes, the hand of the dangling pendulum clock wants me to move forward. What a reminder! This lesson won't be complete if it fails to touch this important part of management decision...

Managing payments: Who you pay, when you pay, how you pay and what you pay could determine the success or failure of your business.

If you must succeed in business you must get this right. Your payment decision determine the degree of your business growth. Be diligent in managing payments or you lock your business in "crisis", let your payment be fair, timely and courteous.

Managing staff payments: More than 55% of a critical analysis of 50 businesses that crumbled revealed that the cause of business failures were due to bad management decision in terms of staff welfare, says

London Economic Analyst- John Learn.

Listen, late payment of salaries, under- payment and hostility on the staff never helped any business to achieve its target.

If you want to maximize profit and the growth of your business, the welfare of your employees should be of utmost importance. It should be considered along side with profitability.

Secret No. 13

Always make good management decision, the growth of your business depends on it.

Secret No. 14

Staff welfare should be considered alongside with profitability.

Pay yourself

Did you hear that? You are also a member of the staff. Remember that your business is a separate entity. You should understand your position as a staff and your due salary. Your business should be able to pay you just like other staff.

You are once reminded that your family depends on your salary not on your business. You must confine your personal expenses within your pocket (your salary). If your salary is $200 per month please live within your reach. You should avoid conflict between "you" and "your business". Don't forget to follow your business plan, but give room for improvement.

It was really a fulfilled day. As I lifted my face, I remembered that we were still on the fifth rung of the ladder . Now the sixth!

LESSON 6

APPLY FINANCIAL WISDOM IN BUSINESS

The difference between a success and a failure may not be lack of money for business but lack of wisdom in business. Even when they have the same information, wisdom makes the difference.

The Scripture says, "Wisdom is profitable to direct " (Ecc. 1 0:10b) .This statement is all encompassing and valid at all time. Your business wants you to invest your financial wisdom.

Money comes to everybody but wisdom retains it in somebody's hand. How much you are able to utilize your wisdom in co-ordinating your financial investments in business determines what you have. Apply financial wisdom! This is the sixth rung the ladder of business creation. Yes, the sixth rung!

I remembered one amazing thing that morning... The class was just about to start; the weather was so bright - one could hardly believe it was still rainy season. What a dazzling sun rays that penetrated the class room! One more thing, there was uniformity in the students' attire. Not in the colour anywhere, but in the class of dress they wore. All were corporately dressed. Well tailored-suits and plain shirts with shoes to march.

The students looked very important and responsible in their corporate attires. They looked like managers. Or was it that I saw managers in them?

Corporate! That was it... My vision was expanding. The new vision hit my mind in a rhema like a missile. I nodded with satisfaction as I looked at them the second time (I caught the vision).

Thank you God for making the pioneers good pace-setters. I also had more reasons to thank God. He gave me the strength to manage all the classes with ease. No one could believe that one person could run all the classes. I couldn't either. But, God made it possible.

I felt the awesome presence of God in my business. The first proof that He was in my business was that He always provided, He also crowned it with good health. The sixth rung of the ladder of business creation marks the end of the first session (first academic year). As our culture, we acknowledged God and began the day's business.

APPLYING FINANCIAL WISDOM

"Wisdom is profitable to direct", is an unforgettable

Scriptural verse. It is important to point out that wisdom is not limited to a particular area of business, but is needed in all aspects... Hence, you must be diligent when it has to do with money.

You should learn business financing. The knowledge is important because the application is inevitable for your business success. Remember that wisdom is simply the application of knowledge. Knowledge is by itself futile without a moving force called wisdom.

Apply your financial wisdom in the following areas: (a) records (b) profit (c) Income (d) expenditure (e) Assets acquisition /investment.

KEEPING RECORDS

Keeping records can resurrect a dead business while lack of records can kill the most enterprising business in the city.

Secret No. 15

This is called the top secret of financial wisdom:

If you want your business to grow, keep records of every financial involvement in your business. Not even a jolt should escape in your record.

Make sure you write down in details all (no matter how small) financial involvements of your business. Not even a dime should come in or go out of your business without passing through your record. Sounds impossible, yet achievable.

Secret No. 16.

You should be accountable through your record in the running of your business. Your record should be able to say something positive at the end of your accounting period.

I had expected questions before now but Jeff raised his hand to ask the first question. "Keeping records of all financial involvements of a business will be all hell of stress. Or don't you think so sir?" "Stress you said; yes stress with success, but think of a stress free failure", I answered looking somewhat passionate.

Business is not leisure, it is work. Don't expect something to happen if you don't want to work, because out of sweat comes sweet. Sweat here doesn't mean struggling, it means work. Yeah!

The students stared at me as I explained; but Jeff seemed to still have one more thing.

"... But what is an accounting period?". Good ! You

should learn to take stock of your business activities and evaluate them financially from time to time. It could be weekly, monthly, quarterly or yearly depending on the type of business you are involved in. This exercise will help you know the growth or otherwise of your business. "The period of this evaluation is the accounting period", I explained.

"You can't do without records if you want to succeed in business", I asserted in a louder voice.

Record Your Profits

This is business (work) not leisure as you think. Profitability is the prime objective. You must have an account book that will always expose your balance sheet to your very eyes. Know in facts and figures how much you make in your business - this helps you to plan better.

Your Income and Expenditure

Your income and expenditure should be readily accessible. Income is the inflows while expenditure is the outflows (in gross terms). Nothing should be excluded not even the "peanut" you bought or one shilling debt you were paid.

Financial wisdom teaches you to be conscious of the fact that your income side must exceed your expenditure side for you to still be in business.

Assets acquisition /Investment

Your financial wisdom is highly needed here. It is not all about acquiring assets, it is in knowing the right assets to acquire. Neither is it in investing in business but knowing what, how and when to invest. All these call for the application of financial wisdom. Be wise, and never dabble ignorantly into acquiring an unprofitable assets or invest wrongly in business. Your financial wisdom will keep you at a safe side.

As much as you take business risks, you should guide it with wisdom - this is the essence of the application of financial wisdom.

You may ask yourself these questions:

* Is this an asset ?

* What would likely be the yield?

* Should I invest?

* Why, when, how?

* What amount is needed?

* Is it worth acquiring or investing on?

Don't risk blindly and foolishly but remember that business excellence depends on right application of financial wisdom.

"What if one fails to apply financial wisdom. What will be the risk ?", Nic asked.

The risk is what you have been trying to avoid... (Yes, business failure). It is like praying "Please God destroy my business, I want to go home".Talking to them: I said, "I think that is an incredible prayer!" (they laughed).

The laughter hung on their checks as I announced their next exam.

LESSON 7

THE VITAL PROS AND CONS

Quite amazing! These were the two most appropriate words that described the outcome of the exam that morning.

There were great improvements. Yes, "excellent"

could be another right word.

All the students were more than average (beyond the mediocre level). Their performance was laudable.

I was overwhelmed not particularly because of the performance of the pioneer class but because other classes were equally wonderful. I saw geniuses emerging from the business creation school. The economy of the nation and the world is about to witness a great positive change, was a voice of confidence which dropped down my mind.

You are on your way to creating business capable of leaving you in opulence. You must conquer these six odds and discover the seven allies that will take you to the place of your dream.

THE STENCH CONS

An author said, "Know your limits and ignore them". But I tell you, know the enemies of business creation and conquer them. This is the most assured way your can get to your destination.

Fear: The most dangerous enemy of business creation is fear. (This enemy held Nic down for many years without daring any business). Fear simply means: Feeling Exploits Aren't Realizable. It is only a feeling but can keep one down forever.

Fear says: Don't! You will not succeed! Fear has a lot of reasons to discourage you and sit you at a spot. But you have a way of escape. It is faith!

Listen to Billy Sunday, "Fear knocked at my door, faith answered... And there was no one there". Good! Have you seen, nobody was there. It was only a feeling!

Fear comes in different forms - fear of failure, fear of starting, fear of criticism, fear of mistakes, fear of size/stature/position etc. William Winglesworth gives us the solution, "When fear knocks at your door, send faith to open the door".

Faith is the antidote! You can learn more on how to crush your fears from one of my books, "Success Dynamics- the Magnate".

I knew that Nic needed to get this part right more than any other student. I had earlier recommended that book to him (you may also need it)

Negativism

It is not possible, it is not true, I cannot, it won't work... Negativism places your mind on the impossible side. The sub-conscious mind is built with negative pillars. This invariably affects the way one thinks and lives.

Negativism makes one think of business failures, not success; loss, not profit. It has a lot of ugly pictures to discourage one.

* Accident

* Theft / Robbery

* Death

* Fire outbreak

*It reminds you of other business failures. "You won't succeed either", it tells you.

It makes you believe you would end in one of the aforementioned pictures. But that is not true. You can do all things through Christ who strengthens you. "With God all things are possible". You'll succeed!

Feed your sub-conscious mind with positive affirmations. Believe you can do exploits. God has made it so and His will supersedes other opinions.

Bad Habit

Bad habit is the killer of destiny. It crushes business ambition and nails it to futility. Many people answer "ex-business men" because of bad and uncontrolled habits.

Bad habits are not only dangerous but frustrating. Have a close look at these:

* Make money in the day, spend it with women in an hotel.

* Make money in four hours, engage in gambling for the next four hours.

* Make money in the day, render account to a bar attendants in the evening.

* While in business take permission to take hard drugs in an hour interval .

* Hire staff today , fire staff tomorrow .

This list could go endless; but they form major reasons for business failures.

Charles R. Swindoll has this to say about habit, "Habit is a cable we weave a thread of it everyday, and at last we cannot break it". Bad habit is hard to break, but the grace of God is the solution. Ask God to help you overcome it if you want your business to rise again.

Slothfulness

Slothfulness keeps some people permanent on the receiving side. They like hard work but wouldn't like to be the hard worker.

If you desire sweet, then you must go for the sweat. Business is sweat which leads to sweet. Every good thing comes out of effort. Business is work, not leisure.

You have the options - to work or to die in hunger. The Scripture says, "He who fails to work should not eat". Dignity of labour.

Have this at the back of your mind -it will push you to work because you would definitely like to eat...

Low Self - Esteem

You are a product of your thought. Many people never worth something because they never think they worth anything. You wonder why some people remain in a particular low status in business for an indefinite time, it is simply because they esteem themselves low - incapable of doing something extra- ordinary.

You are what you think. A renowned philosopher Rene Descartes posited, "I think therefore I am". The scripture has made the verdict even before this assertion: it says, "As a man thinketh in his heart so is he" (Proverbs 23:7).

Esteem yourself fit and capable to do business and excel!

Imitation

Many businesses crumble because they are mere imitations. They have no foundation but are built on other people's pattern. Another word for this is "copying" . This act limits business growth and frustrates business creation. John Mason says, "Imitation is limitation".

The best way to be viable in business is to be unique. Make your own impression. business creation answers to originality. Imitation is the opposite of originality.

Don't be a copy-cat, think of a new way- your own way.

If you can overcome these stench you are on your way to creating an invaluable business, I told the students.

There are also some insights that will take you to your destination. Let me introduce them to you.

THE VITAL PROS

Now that you have overcome the stench cons, here are seven pros that will place you on your target.

Creative idea

Your creative idea makes you original, not an imitation. Distinguish yourself by doing it in your own way. Business is a product of creative idea. You can start with your small idea. A best-seller wealth creation author - Robert Kiyosaki asserts, "Every self- made person started small with idea, then turned it into something big".

Plan

Business heads nowhere without plan. Plan is the

compass which directs your business. Your plan reveals your strategies and gets you focused until your dream comes true. "Plan increases self confidence and assures profitability", I quite agree with A.S. Emmanuel. Remember that plan is the foundation of a business, you can't avoid it.

Enthusiasm

Enthusiasm gives you a fast result in business. If you add zeal to your business, it will give you an amazing result. Build your mind with what will motivate you to work hard.

Determination

Don't think of going back, "Forward ever, backward never". Be poised to make it. Persevere if it delays. "Never say 'never' " says John Mason. It can't be over until you hit your target. Never give up!

Confidence

This is a virtue which will help your business to attain your target height. Never doubt your ability. Don't think that your product or idea is not satisfactory . Look at your business idea as a world-class. Advertise it with confidence and positive mind set. It will make a difference.

Ingenuity

Be smart in your actions. Think smart! Business is a product of thought. Think of finding a solution to a problem -that is business for you. Distinguish your business with your intelligent plan.

Diligence

Diligence crowns all your efforts with success. Business is not done "any how" it is done "somehow".

You may need to follow business ethics to ensure profitability. First thing first; the right thing at the right time! Ensure harmony in your business. "Seeth thou a man diligent in his business; he shall stand before kings...", Proverbs 22:9. I sincerely recommend these seven friends to you if you want to create business capable of making you live big and fulfilled. "Thank you sir!", the students chorused (I could see smiles of satisfaction). Smile radiated...

Secret No. 17

Overcome fear, negativism, bad habits, laziness, low-self-esteem and imitation. Work with creative idea, plan enthusiasm, determination, confidence, ingenuity and diligence. These are sure-bets for business creation.

LESSON 8

INVESTMENT IS KEY

Is this the key you know? Good! This is an important level in your quest to build your dream business...Without investment, business creation becomes as barren as "the fig tree". But wait a minute...

I know you would like to remind me the appointment with the commissioner, I still remember (it is next week); I said as I poured a cupid smile... The students were surprised at my words.

"Sir, are you a Sanguine?", Matt asked. "Sanguine?" I retorted.. (I knew he was talking

about temperament but was surprised he was bring that). But, am I a Sanguine?

"Yes or no or just a little blend? Dominant Mel... And a blend of chol... (We should hold it there to avoid further distraction).

Some of the students got me highly elated during the week - Dan and Chizo almost got one hundred percent in all the courses. In fact they deserved 100% but I didn't want them to feel they had arrived and relax. I still wanted them to do something better. I boldly wrote on their scripts, "Your work is impressive, but don't relax -work harder !"

I also remembered that Julie's performance in her first exam was similar to what I saw. As I ruminated, my mind was fast to capture the future. The society would soon be transformed. Business would blossom like never before; success shall overtake failure and the school shall perfect its name (business creation school). A dream shall become a reality! Wow! We must hit it big!

Who thinks of harvest without sowing? (I went back to the topic -hitting it from behind). Investment is inevitable in wealth creation....

WHY INVEST?

One of the major objectives of a business is profitability. Profit is therefore a product of investment. To realize this golden objective, it is pertinent to invest ... Invest!

Your target is the future not the past

You have a plan which takes you to your target. Your

dream is not going back to yesterday, but to ensure a pleasant future. It is therefore important to cancel the ugly mistakes (failures) of yesterday by instilling hope to the future - think of investment.

Your business should grow

There is just one sure way to move forward, to overcome stagnation and failure -it is investment. You should know that wealth creation is not alienated from business growth; and business growth comes as a result of investment.

To keep your offsprings when you are dead

"Live big and rich...". You can only be said to have fulfilled your purpose when you have something that will keep your offsprings after several decades of your death.

Physical death is inevitable but you can still live by your impression while you were alive. Your investment creates lasting impression even at your death. Dying fulfilled is all about having godly investments which would speak through generations when you can't be physically seen. Please make an impression in your generation - invest!

Distinguish yourself as a hero

In warfare, victims abound but heroes are mentioned.

Millions of people had come to the world and gone unnoticed, while some people's names remain indelible in the world success hall of fame archive.

Don't be like the people who made no impression in their generation. You should be distinguished a hero in your generation -think of investment (create a lasting impression).

A seed can't bear fruits until it is sown

A seed remains a seed until it is sown. It can never appreciate but can depreciate forever. No one ever reaps the fruits of his harvest without sowing (first).

Investment is like sowing a seed. You should be diligent on what, how, where you invest. You can draw your lesson from the scripture... Sow bountifully if you want to reap bountifully. Your wealth creation reacts to what and how you invest. Let your investment be guided by wisdom (Godly wisdom)

Secret No. 18

Investment is a sure-bet for wealth creation. Be careful on how and where you invest. Your wealth creation depends on your investment.

Secret No. 19

Think of investment if you want to live big and rich or to be distinguish as a hero in your world.

KINGDOM INVESTMENT

Investment is not limited to business. The surest and fastest way to hit your wealth creation target is by "Kingdom investment".

Kingdom investment is laying your treasures in Heaven - this is done by your kingdom commitments here on earth - through tithing, offering, supporting church projects/works and giving other free-will offerings.

This is one of the most striking things I have ever mentioned in this book. I know many readers would say "Hooo hoo! What?", just like Jeff. But I won't like you to miss out (this is the whole truth). Remember, "God is the wealth creator" (Deut. 8: 18). He can give us the power to create wealth . I didn't want to delve more into this because it is in the lesson plan.

#Secret No.20 (The Golden Secret)

Kingdom investment is essential for business creation. God is a principal partner..

Secret No 21

The five senses are veritable realms to achieving common goals but the revelational sense transcends common achievements.

Bishop David Oyedepo rightly said, "One revelation from God is worth more than life time of struggles."

I highlighted the points and made the students understand that there is a sense realm where all things are possible. This realm I believe was described as, "Faith" in Hebrews chapter eleven. Or the subconscious realm in Psychology, or simply as power of imagination. But one thing is sure, it is extraordinary way of reaching out.

LESSON 9

EXPLORE THE SENSE REALM

The sense realm is very vital in business creation. You need to explore it because business success is a smooth interaction of the senses: touch, hearing, smell, taste, sight... Yet, far more productive than the listed five senses is a unique realm which all great achievers explore. This uncommon dimension of achieving business exploits should be considered with utmost diligence because it is the hub of the creative force that makes all things possible.

While we bank on the power of the five senses for common result in business, we explore the revelational sense for uncommon business exploits. Emphasizing the power of the uncommon sense, 1 shared my experiences and explained how this realm can lead to great achievements. I recalled how I was stuck in a tough situation during my undergraduate years. All options common with the five senses realm could not pull me through. Time was tickling and pressure was quite enormous but with my five senses actively in place hope was on the verge of crashing. Suddenly, there was a switch to uncommon realm. It was revelational, infinite and creative. A unique realm of idea with boundless hope and assurance; not even my five senses could believe that what they could not achieve in four years of meticulous work could be achieved within an hour through revelational sense realm (the dynamic faith).

It was an unbelievable experience; my school

fee was released, paid to school account through bank, collected receipt, did all clearance (sports, library, medical, departmental, faculty, students affairs, bursary etc), collected NYSC Call-up letter and my statement of result within an hour. When I boarded a bus in the next hour to catch up with the NYSC orientation which would start the next 24 hours, I had no doubt that I was operating on an uncommon sense platform. I was indeed in-charge and everything I needed came on a platter of my imagination. All I thought about immediately became reality. By the force of faith, every door was open and assistance beckoned. As I narrated my experience, the students were stupefied.

In my diligent study of great men in the success hall of fame, I realized they operated on this uncommon sense realm. Their innovations, inventions, creative prowess and extra-ordinary achievements were not on the (ordinary) five senses realm but a reflection of deep revelational sense beyond the "box" of life and the power to connect the infinite realm.

The Uncommon Sense Realm

This is the anvil where business ideas are laid and formed. I call it the uncommon sense because we concentrate in the use of the five senses we know (sense of sight, taste, touch, smell and hearing), but don't explore this unique sense realm. Call it the sixth sense or number six, the uncommon sense is a deeper, higher, wider and more result oriented realm of reaching out. It is a vision pack. Little wonder Helen Keller though blind said, "The worst form of blindness is having sight without vision". There is no doubt vision is the pathway for revelational sense. Where the five senses cannot prevail, revelational sense transcends. Yes, deeper meditation and imagination place us on this unique platform in business creation.

"Use your number six!" My teacher charged me in my early school years when he thought I had exhausted my five senses options but he still believed l had a chance to reach out to success, "out of the box".

His voice reverberated in me and caused me to transcend the uncommon sense realm. And just then, I connected... I got it right.

Business creation resides in this realm and it is generated by switching on your imagination on the creative horizon.

Lesson Seventeen of this book thoroughly explained how to achieve this target. You will uncover the unique pathway to reaching your business and career dreams.

Beyond the Five Senses

The five senses realm may be the right platform on different stages in business creation but outstanding business exploits go beyond these (ordinary) realms.

You must dig deep to connect the extra- ordinary reality through revelational sense. Skew your mind positively to think, to meditate, to imagine infinite possibilities... Until you move your inspiration to a boundless zone where you can create your world and be the answer to myriads of questions unanswered, your influence and net-worth will not manifest. This is the time to explore... A trip beyond the five senses.

* Get answers to uncommon questions

* Generate idea to create business

* Connect the supernatural realm

* Faith may be all you need to apply.

LUN SAGE

LESSON 10

MAKE TEAM A HABIT

Every leading business is a synergy, network or successful interpersonal relationship. It means for a business to be a selling brand, it must directly or indirectly gather inputs from different persons. The idea may come from one person who takes credit for the invention, innovation or exploit but the input of other persons in the process cannot be undermined. As we progress in this lesson, you will discover one of the healthy attitudes which stirs rapid business success.

I recalled an African proverb, "If you want to go fast, go alone. If you want to go far, go together." I smiled and asked rhetorically: What is the need going fast to nowhere?

An idea may come from one person but the synergy of a team makes it a leading brand. Therefore, the success of a business is the combination of efforts of persons at various levels, locations and times invested to advance a viable idea of someone. I laid emphasis on the fact that someone cannot successfully push an idea to global limelight without the inputs of other persons at various stages. I hinted that the regular office works we engage in daily underscore the relevance of teamwork. I paused and recounted my past job experience.

My Banking Experience

I spent the first seven years of my career as an employee in the banking industry. It was an unforgettable experience for me in so many ways. Remembering the bank major segments: the operation and marketing departments. I was in the later. Marketing in the banking industry was a serious business. Damn challenging. Your "figures" would prove your worth. It was a teamwork, yet individual performance was highly emphasized. The ability of a sales staff to meet his/her target ensures his/her stay and possible promotion. In the midst of the tough situation, I discovered that the priority of the bank was for the marketing department to meet or surpass its target...

In one of the branches where I worked, a formidable strategy to consistently meet the target was initiated by the branch management. That required the application of one business healthy attitudes which is the focus of this lesson -the teamwork.

We were trained to work as a team and handed a slogan, "Together everyone achieves more (TEAM)".

We had common goal and strategy. We always noted our challenges and looked for ways to handle them. The synergy was so cordial that the strong became the pillar for the weak. There was maximum understanding as we engaged in internal training and re-training. Most times we moved out in group (team) to make presentations in big institutions and establishments. A member of the team would facilitate another member would backup, while others would be involved in guiding prospective customers fill relevant forms and documents.

The Team Power

Yes, we made it! The outcome was impressive. Our branch moved from struggling branch to a profit making branch and was able to sustain its healthy status for many months until something happened. Something dramatic changed the tide. But prior to that

„ not only did the branch make profit, all the team members had good performance. The least was average. Consequently, the Team Lead was promoted and sent for special training. The choice of a new Team Lead tore the team because the branch management and the other team members differed. At last the branch management decided to allow marketers focus on their individual targets. That was it! Within the period, some marketers actually surpassed their targets. Others were far below average. Then, the branch performance nosedived. All the performance indices dropped. Consistently they did. Do you know why?

In our general analysis and appraisal, we discovered that the healthy attitude of teamwork has great power. Such stunning lesson!

We Engage Attitude Like Team Habit

Yes, team habit makes business a sustained reality. I got to the main insight of this lesson by redefining wealth (my own inspired way). The new definition was to explore the inner worth (self worth) and the relevance of cordial interrelationship for business profitability. I analyzed wealth as an acronym and formed a powerful active statement :

W - We

THE BUSINESS SECRET POWER

E - Engage

A - Attitudes

L - Like

T - Team

H - Habit

When we engage attitudes like team habit, we gain more productivity and profitability because teamwork is the chain which draws the wealth of every business enterprise.

More lines of thought filled my mind. The team interrelationship that brought various global brand: Coca Cola, Adidas, Nokia etc. All shows how someone's idea became a global business (brand) by successive inputs of other people over a period of time.

You need people to express your idea better and bigger. Dr Yonggi Cho's story on my mind.

Dr Yonggi Cho's Experience

I quickly shared the insightful understanding I received from Dr Yonggi Cho through his book, "Successful Home cell Groups". My intention was to drive deeper in their minds the fact that team habit is in deed for every business; not just secular businesses but also for God's business (ministry). It was an apt illustration of the effect of doing business alone and the success reality of a team.

Dr Yonggi Cho is the founder of the Full Gospel Central Church, Seoul, Korea. Acclaimed to be the single largest congregation in the world. God taught him how to substitute personal (egocentric) attitude with the winning attitude of team habit.

Early in his ministry, Dr Cho knew the importance of setting goals and having faith to achieve it. But he believed he was the best tool for God to always use. With the steady increasing number of his congregation, he engaged in preaching, teaching, counseling, water baptism of new converts, Holy Ghost service etc. Eventually, he was struck by life threatening sickness which ravaged his health for over ten years. He earnestly called on God for healing. When Dr Cho was finally healed by God; and he bagged a grave lesson. He learnt that delegation of authority and team habit are in deed approved of God. Consequently, his experience birthed Home Cell Fellowship which has become a global strategy adopted by many congregation to evangelize and expand church network.

Please Get It Right

Your business has a unique identity for maximum success. It is called TEAM. Your team is your power, your connection to your business profit.

Now, list your team members in your business. Think of how to get the best out of them for your maximum profit.

An English Premier League side has the slogan, "Never walk alone" I agree with that. Never walk alone! Be a team player!

Jesus Christ had his team (the twelve disciples) and more. God had his team: Genesis 1:26, "... and God said , let us make man in our own image, after our likeness. And let them have dominion over the fish of the sea and over the fowl of the earth..." In the above scriptural reference, the use of the plural word, "us" indicates the synergy of a team. That was backed up by the repeated use of, "our" to affirm the use of the plural identity in the context. Man is therefore a product of synergy (team) and given power (dominion) - the bye product of the teamwork. Dominion is also the symbol of victory and success.

I hesitated and mused, "If God needed a team to succeed in His business, why do you think you can win alone?"

The teamwork is the right attitude and pathway for business exploits

LESSON 11

YOUR MENTALITY MATTERS

The students were gradually becoming conscious of their destination. Their attire told me. Corporately gorgeous. It was as if they were already prepared for this lesson. Do you think it is possible to live above the string of poverty?

You can be accessed here and now. If your answer is "Yes", congratulations! You are on the right track... But if your answer is "No", Oh oh! (You missed out). But you can get it right again. You can connect... Be positively skewed.

You are what you believe, in order words a product of your own thought. Didn't you hear the scripture say, "As a man thinketh in his heart so is he" (Prov. 23:7)? What you need is the right mind positioning - to accept positives and reject negativesj.

Matt, Jeff and Nic were about having the privilege of a unique concept in business creation.

Have you ever pondered on the damn scourge of

poverty? Poverty! Were you able to trace its root or its solution? Do you know your mentality matters on this subject matter?

POVERTY IS A SIEGE

Poverty is not just lack of money; it is lack of privileges, pleasures and treasures in God's plan for mankind. The most miserable type of poverty is living without the fear of God. Without God, man is a pauper!

In business creation, poverty mentality is low initiative or creative ideas that generates exploits.

DEALING WITH POVERTY

You can never overcome poverty by your wish but by a practical application of knowledge, wisdom and understanding inspired by God or through learning.

Have this understanding; poverty mentality is dangerous... For you to be outstanding, you must wear a rich mind-set. Think of the right steps and strategies. This battle is first fought in the mind and victory delivered through work in the physical realm.

* Empower your mind positively: What you think is

what you are! Empower your mind to reject poverty. Stop thinking poor! Look at the best as what you deserve. Poverty is very sensitive just like success. Whereas poverty flows to the negative and pessimistic direction of thinking, success follows the positive and optimistic direction of thought. Even when poverty is close and certain, it can be averted by the positive positioning of the mind. This fact has been proved true time without number. During the early ministry of Kenneth Copeland, he looked like an exemplified piece of poverty - everything around him smelt "poor", but he kept on confessing success and diligently working on his God given ministry. It is an indisputable fact that he became one of the most successful preachers in the world. Bishop David O. Oyedepo is another living example. People thought he was only a joker when he started saying, "I can never be poor!" What he confessed was contrary to what people were seeing... But his confession later prevailed. No matter the yardstick for success and great achievement, he is in deed a success. His name has been boldly written in the world success hall of fame.

Examples of people who turned their destinies from poverty to success abound - they are also in your neighbourhood.

Poverty is a product of thought. Your mentality status

defines your position. If you want success in business, change your thought pattern. Think right, think wide!

Say it!

The physical realm may feign ignorant of the activities of the spiritual realm until it is communicated to. Don't only have it in mind - say it! Speak to yourself; not as a mad man, but as a sane man who knows where he is going and what he is doing. The word of God says that you are rich, affirm it: say "I am rich!". Share your positive thought with others wisely especially to those who will encourage you in the area of your dream.

Express yourself!

Speak about it not boastfully, but as the discovering of your kingdom covenant heritage. Keep your thought alive-confess it! (Be guided by wisdom).

Wit and wisdom say, "You will never be a success until you train your mind to be success conscious" . The words of Napoleon Hill is still fresh, "There is no limitation to the mind except those we acknowledge". He further asserted, "Both poverty and riches are the offspring of thought". Zig Ziglar summed if up thus, "What you picture in your mind, your mind will go to work to accomplish, when you change your pictures you automatically change yourself".

Have a Goal

Aim at something; you must desire something great. Have a definite target of what you want or where you are going. Business doesn't come anyhow, it is aimed at ... Define your goal and pursue it. Life without a goal has no locus and no direction. Define your goal now!

Plan

Career or business creation doesn't just come by thinking and confessing positively or by having a target. There must also be a well laid plan to achieve what you think, confess and dream. Plan activates the trio for an onward transmission. Plan through your vision how to turn your status of poor mental servitude to rich creativity.

Your Idea Is A Resource

An idea is like the mustard seed - small as it could appear, but the biggest of all. Idea is the king of all the resources that can generate your business growth. In your plan, invest your idea into your dream business. Never think that your idea is small, inferior or not good enough.

Explore The Horizon...

Go Extra, Do Extra!

Remember, your goal here is to generate business empire. Be ready for tireless mental engagement.

Do extra thinking, planning and working and go extra to make sure you hit your target. It is when extra is added to ordinary that great exploits are achieved. Be unlimited creative... Recognize God's Grace

God empowered us with grace. He endowed us to explore the abundance of life. God's gift of righteousness wins it all. Jesus Christ makes things beautiful. Your ability to connect to this grace gives the needed access to unlimited providence.

God is the author of destinies. Don't fight as if it is by your strength. The scripture says, "It is not by strength that any man should boast," again it says, "It is neither of him that runneth nor of him that willeth, but of God that showeth mercy." Recognize His grace for business exploits.

"Grace" is what keeps you. Remember that the letter 'G' is the most important letter in the word "Grace". 'G' designates God. Without the 'G' (God factor) you are just in a "race" (struggle). Struggling (depicts mediocrity.

Deut. 8:18, "But thou shall remember the Lord thy

God: for it is he that giveth power to make wealth…"

MIND YOUR BUSINESS!

Having empowered your vision through your idea, mind your business knowing that you are not destined to end a mediocre but a success. Never allow slothfulness in your business. Focus is the right platform for profitability.

* Save

* Invest wisely.

Watch your Expenditure

Don't spend more than you earn. Be diligent in your expenditure especially at the beginning of your business. If you want to be announced by the size of your balance sheet of business. Spend wisely especially at the out set.

Take Stock!

Make it a habit, access your business periodically. Know the size of your business quantitatively and financially. You could save yourself the stress of going down the line through accurate stock taking.

Secret No. 23

Be positive towards life; empower your mind to visualize a successful career or business empire.

Secret No. 24

Confess what you believe and aim at it through your plan.

Secret No. 25

Without God we would remain in a race (struggle /poverty). We must recognize His G(race) to help us overcome poverty.

Nic asked a very important question. His question practically depicted his society. It is the same question which loom the minds of people daily.

"Why do the rich get richer and the poor get poorer?".

"The rich get richer because their minds are positively tuned for riches. They think rich, plan rich and sees riches. They have consciously made rich habits... And riches can never elude them. The poor also get poorer because poverty has beclouded their thinking faculty: they think poor, plan poor and see low level achievements. "I can always manage", they will tell you". If the poor can think and plan like the rich, he will also become rich. But on the contrary, the poor accepts his status and the rich also accepts his status - each of them tends to the peak - poor, poorer and... The rich, richer ... It is all about mentality that transmutes to reality. The mind programming.

Listen, if the rich man start to think and plan like the poor man, poverty will definitely overtake him viz a viz .

"I am rich !" Nic affirmed. "But not richer than I!" Jeff opposed. "Richer then everybody!", Nic maintained (standing up). Laughs...

The lesson ended on good notes- positive confessions. I had no doubt that God's presence was within. My instinct said so...

Thank you Lord!

LESSON 12

THE RELEVANCE OF MONEY

Money is a desirable power for business expansion! This is where your ingenuity and acumen play their roles. Like the pyramid you know, when money is laced on idea; business can be structured in this amazing pattern. The peak of the pyramid satisfies our target in the journey of business creation - the way to opulence.

In business creation, financial investment is necessary because money repositions business. You can't avoid this concept if you must hit it big. Remember, money is an important complement, not the starting point.

VOICES OF AUTHORITIES

Russ Von hit it strategically, "The Richest people in the world all make use of wealth pyramiding". Brain Koslow held the foundational part, "The very first step in building wealth is to spend less than you make". May be you still need a step down the ladder, Napoleon Hill helps you out, "A positive mental attitude is the starting point of all riches of a material or intangible riches".

One more thing is important before we delve into this subject matter... "If you want more money simply change your thinking", says Robert Kiyosaki

Money multiplies business

Money is the female part of wealth creation; when combine with the male counterpart (idea), it breeds business growth. Money multiplies itself, this act is positively contagious - as such everything around is affected. Business and economic boom are possible.

Money generates more money through business investments. An idle money is as good as a waste. Until you know the right place to invest your money business success remains unattainable.

* Buy Securities: Securities are general terms for all written or printed financial documents by which the claims of holders in specified property are secured. They could be stocks, shares, bonds and debentures traded on the stock exchange market.

Debenture and Bonds: These are kinds of securities (legal documents) representing a promise by a company or government (in case o f a bond) t o pay back a loan plus certain amount of interest over a definite period of time. Shares and Stock: A Share is a unit in a capital structure of a business. Stock and share represent ownership interest in a business.

To invest and trade on these securities you need the services of experts (e.g. Stock brokers). It is however not wise to start trading on securities at the early part of a business because some securities take long time for benefits to be recouped.

Your money can make money by buying securities sellable at a later date for a high yield (interest or dividend).

Invest in high yielding Assets

Money can make money through the application of financial wisdom in investment. Financial wisdom gives you the positive result. Invest in high yielding assets especially those that always appreciate. Think of investment, think of high yielding assets.

Land

It is a wise investment decision to acquire or purchase

land. The cost of land is ever in the increase. The cost of a plot of land worth $10,000 this year is possible to increase by subsequent years. Because land appreciates steeply upwards, you could hit your business target by buying land sellable at a later date.

Real estate

This is another place to invest. Just like land, the value of house also appreciate. Even if a house is old or dilapidated, it could still go for an amazing sum of money because it is occupying a (land) space which is an asset of its own.

Generally, landed property generates money that multiplies itself and creates an inestimable returns.

Gold and other precious stones

Those who trade on gold never regretted it. This is because the price of gold appreciates in value. You can invest your money in assets that have high appreciating power like gold, diamond and other precious stones.

"Wisdom is profitable to direct..." This scriptural quotation should always be your watch word. Don't dabble into any business investment with the mind-set of hitting it big without first understanding it... You can also invest in other precious stones (silver, diamond etc). But learn the "where", "how" and "why"...

Business turn-over

This is a very fast way of making your money make more money. It is strongly recommended especially when money is just introduced in a business that involves tangible goods. Fast business turn-over builds business and multiplies money.

*Takes business creation from a low horizon to a high horizon.

*It grows business from ordinary to extra- ordinary.

*It takes business exploits to the peak.

*Money generates more money rapidity.

*It makes business target a possibility.

*Gives a business a new identity .

MONEYAND BUSINESS GROWTH

Business growth is viable with money but deficient without money.

Money is a servant that performs the most difficult task, runs all errands and delivers all results

Money is a servant, yet very intelligent that it masters all languages. Alphra was therefore right when he said, "Money speaks the language all nations understand"

Money is not only a servant in wealth creation but also a servant in all things at all time. This is exactly the implication of the statement by King Solomon, " Money answereth all things..." Money has secret powers and delivers desired results.

Your idea is the mastermind, money is the servant. It only masters all things such that it could run errands for all who would send it. This the platform where business is created.

Secret No. 25

The richest people in the world all make use of wealth pyramiding. Apply wisdom, use money to grow your business fortune.

Do your best all the time

High achievers look at the word "best" as progressive but how achievers look at it as static. After hitting extra-ordinary exploits, a high achiever doesn't relax there he looks for another possible higher place. But a low achiever relaxes immediately he emerges a winner.

Business success gives you the status of a high achiever;

do your best, give your best... Yet don't look at your best but look for yet 'the best' (make room for improvement).

Harvey Firestone alarmed, "You get the best out of others when you give the best of yourself".

Secret No. 26

You can use money to make money by buying shares, stocks, bonds debenture, landed property, gold and other jewelry re-sellable at a later date for higher returns.

Secret No. 27

Money is a servant, but masters 'all' things. Use it to generate your wealth.

Before the end of the lesson Matt asked the same question which boggled my mind many years ago, before I understood the secrets of money and wealth creation.

"Why is money so important?" He asked (smiles). Money is so important because of its function and value (smiles again)... It is the value God assigns to anything that determines its importance. God created money as an instrument with a multi-purpose task to accomplish. It has been proved over and again that money is the answer to most life problems. This calls for its importance (because that is what it is) - servant of all"

LESSON 13

GOOD ASSETS MANAGEMENT TECHNIQUE

It was interesting to discover one striking thing - the society is becoming conscious of the need for acquisition of knowledge. Not just ordinary knowledge but business creation knowledge. Some decades past, many people especially some religious sects were beclouded with the damned mentality that they could only enjoy riches in Heaven. They believed that being rich depicts unrighteousness; as such they ignore an important aspect of God redemption plan for mankind.

Thank God for the new breeze of change and awakening to the knowledge of the truth and understanding of the mind and thought of God concerning His people. God wants us to prosper, both in the body, spirit and soul.

*   His blessings are our inheritance - Duet. 28:1-12.

*   Jesus became poor that we might be rich-2 Corinthians 8:9.

*   God gave us power to make wealth Duet. 8:18.

*   We should possess wealth and riches Gen.8:22.

It is the will of God for us to have this declaration which is a voice of abundance "My lines are fallen unto me in pleasant places; yeah, I have a good heritage" (Psalm 16:6).

It is only the truth that makes free . The students should know the truth which will help them grow their business, having performed excellently in all their exams... The thirteen rung in the academic calender marks a remarkable limelight in business. It also marks a step higher from the level of mediocrity towards higher exploits. Great!

Assets management is essential as business creation would be incomplete without it...

YOU HAVE ASSETS!

Thinking of good assets management would be easier when you know you have them. You can only protect and preserve what you have. It is not always how well you manage other peoples assets but how well you manage your assets that distinguishes your business. You have assets - these assets produce other assets that help you to hit your target.

PHASE ONE Mental or Intellectual Assets

This is the origin and source of other assets. "I think, therefore I am ", said a renowned Philosopher -Rene Descartes.

God gives us the power to create wealth through the right application of our mental (intellectual) assets.

Think well, plan well and use wisdom to pursue your dream. Manage your mental assets well to generate excellence. You can be what you want to be, but don't cage yourself with negative mental attitude.

Your potential is a unique asset

Potential is a unique asset you have which can give you all you desire. Your potential distinguishes you in the place of your exploits.

When business creation is targeted at without potential, it ends in frustration and futility. Take time to discover your potential and do well to align your career to it.

Business is easier to create when your potential is in harmony with your choice career... When a movie actor chooses to be a Pastor, the Pulpit will turn a stage and the Pew his spectators.

Your potential is an asset - the raw material which generates your business. It is never inferior ... But can make you the greatest in your generation.

Idea

This is an asset which may come in little drop, but could be expanded beyond the limits of imagination. Idea gives answers and shows the way forward in wealth creation. Your idea can work an amazing thing if you can develop it. It could be the sure way for your success creation. You can learn how to work on your idea through the diligent process in lesson seventeen (Maximize Your Idea).

Virtue

Virtue is an asset which speaks good things about you. It speaks for you when you are not there.

Think of virtue, think of:

* Integrity

* Honesty

* Charisma

* Accountability

Virtue is an asset which makes you to be remembered and rewarded. Virtue has made many people rich through reward out of their good works.

PHASE TWO

* Liquid Asset

Liquid Asset is money or that which can easily be converted to money. Money is important in business creation and in the growth of an economy.

How well you manage your money largely determines the size of your balance sheet at the end of a business year and at your old age ... Money should be handled with wisdom especially in the investment process. It is to be enjoyed, but not to be wasted. With money, think of productivity and profitability. These invariably gives you the comfort you desire.

Good financial management makes money make more money and business creation attainable.

* Acquired Assets

These are other assets which are created from the assets you already have. Each of the assets mentioned can create business, but liquid asset could make it faster.

* Securities

* Landed property

* Machineries etc.

Good management of these assets distinguishes you and establishes business success.

Secret No. 29

Your assets enhances business growth. Good assets management makes business profitable.

Secret No. 30

Potential, intelligence, idea, virtue, money, securities etc are assets which should be efficiently managed to enhance business success.

Top Secret Power!

"Commit your ways unto the Lord and He will direct your path..." A right step with God gives you the wisdom for assets management.

I was sure that God was perfecting my plans... The performance, co-operattion, discipline and zeal from the students were so amazing. Things were naturally peaceful and in perfect harmony. All the students now dress corporate (impeccable). The society has a bright future.

"One secret from Heaven is worth more than a whole

lifetime of struggles" - David O. Oyedepo

LESSON 14

BUSINESS LONEVITY HAS DIVINE PRINCIPLES

In the fourteenth rung of the business ladder! This lesson was like a flavour... I was amazed at the students' expressions; it was as if an energizer was dropped down their spirits - they were inspired and couldn't hide that possible fact.

Could it be because they had much interest in their business longevity. Their smiles were bold almost erupting into a convulsing laughter. Nic couldn't stifle his when it plugged out; the sign still spread on his check. It could be a sign of positive affirmation!

I must hit it big! From the registered interest of the members of the society the dream school was going to start formally with over one thousand students in a good learning environment. All the students had done their plan, half of the number may not have the initial capital to activate their plans. I would help them raise money for onward creation of their dream business by employing them to teach in the business creation school. I would pay them handsomely. Interesting!

We would re-build the economy together ... And hit our business targets!

OLD AGE SYNDROME

It's a common believe that old age is a time to be dependent, because of the weakness of the body systems. Body systems could be weak due to old age, but exploits could be at its climax.

A hackneyed wise saying flashed my mind, I should use it to buttress this fact. "The fire-wood fetched during the dry season warms the fire-place during the rainy season".

Old age is not being dependent financially or in building business. Your early business creation strategy and investment can make you financially independent at your old age (spilling to several decades after your death).

THE SECRETS

Planning is an important element of success! Getting richer even at old age is planned for, it doesn't come by accident but through deliberate engagements.

1. Have Godly beginning

Every business with godly foundation makes great difference. The scripture says, "It is the blessing of God that maketh rich and addeth no sorrow". True riches can only be created by God, but can be counterfeited by the devil. Every fake thing is temporary but God's acts are eternally satisfying.

The first secret of enjoying lasting business success is laying your foundation on God.

Can you now realize a possible reason many people become extremely rich and successful at their youth but extremely poor in their old age. If you want to have a pleasant old age, begin your business with God! Godly beginning ends well!

2. Good investment decisions

Investment is like sowing a seed... Good investment decision is like sowing on a good soil.

Apply wisdom when you want to invest, what you recoup in your business depends on the quality of your investment decision. Enrich your old age by taking quality decisions in your business investment (now).

3. Avoid Debts

As much as possible avoid borrowing especially when

your business turn-over cannot meet up with the amount borrowed. Much borrowing could lead to bad debt which could make life miserable at old age.

Business don't always flourish because of the large volume of money, but because of the right application of business principles.

4. Plan your home

Build a responsible home with Godly principles. No man can enjoy his old age if his family is at war or in disarray and no amount of money/ wealth can last in the hands of hoodlums. If you want your wealth to last and your old age to be stress-free, you must raise a responsible home -instill peace, harmony and respect for one another.

5. Work With Rules

Rules instill harmony. Set rules as instruments that guide your home and business. Your business is both for your present family and for some generations to come; it is not for the survival of the fittest, but a standard to be emulated. Your family should add value to your business and build their own business.

Instill quest for independence in your home so that they could explore and create their own business.

Support exploits initiated by your children or family members. Help them to stand on their own -by this act you are making them independent and planning the growth of your business at your old age will be possible.

Teach them the rules that made you successful and guide them to apply same. Let there be order in the management of your business.

6. Help Others

Getting richer even at old age? Don't be selfish, this dream could also be possible through the help you rendered to others. If you damn the bridge you plied on your way up, it could be your only option on your way home (old age). The help you rendered to people can make your old age the fortune of your dream.

The scripture alarms, "Cast your bread upon the waters after many days you will find it..." (Ecc. 11:1-2). There is always a good reward for a good deed!

7. Invest in the God's Kingdom

Kingdom investment is like putting your treasure in a safe store-house for your use now, during your old age and eternity. But more than what the store-house can do, it is close to the returns in bank fixed deposit... Yet more, it multiplies your investment even at your old age. Kingdom investment is done in the church by paying all financial obligations and by supporting the work of God.

It is the plan of God for us to flourish even in our old age... Your business success should not be limited by age. God said in his word, " The righteous shall flourish like the palm tree, and grow like a Cedar in Lebanon. They are planted in the house of the Lord, they flourish in the Courts of our God. They still bring forth fruit in old age, they are ever full of sap and green" (Psalms 92:2-14).

Secret No. 31

Kingdom investment can stimulate business longevity.

Secret No. 32

Have a Godly beginning, make good investment decisions, plan your home, help others... Are the sure ways to enjoy business longevity.

Secret No. 33

Make your own impact. Let opulence stimulate unlimited business success. Don't block business flow channel.

DIVINE BUSINESS SECRETS

The secrets and principles of business success are found in the Scripture: Job 22:21-29

- Acquaint now thyself with him and be at peace: thereby good shall come unto thee.

- Receive I pray thee, the law from his mouth and lay up his words in thine heart.

- If thou return to the Almighty, thou shall be built up, thou shall put away iniquity far from thy tabernacles.

- Then shall thou lay up gold as dust, and the gold of Ophir as the stones of the brooks.

- Yea, the Almighty shall be thy defense, and thou shall have plenty of silver.

- For thou shall have thy delight in the Almighty, and shall lift up thy face unto God.

- Thou shall make thy prayer unto him, and he shall hear thee, and thou shall pay thy vow.

- Thou shall also decree a thing and it will be established unto thee, and light shall shine upon thy way.

- When men are cast down, then thou shall say, there

is a lifting up; and he shall save the humble person.

LESSON 15

BUSINESS SUCCESS BRINGS RESPONSIBILITIES

Don't run away, don't give excuses.business success brings responsibilities. This rung of the ladder of business creation gets you to know the purpose of business acquisition.

This is very important because when the purpose of a thing is not known abuse is inevitable.

Be responsible! Winston Church Hill asserted, "The price of greatness is responsibility".

Don't ask for it if you are not ready to pay the price. If you are not responsible with your business success, it means you are not qualified to have it.

I reflected on a story: a man made an amazing invention. The demand for his product was high... He made over $5,000 on the first month of his invention.

The second month was also inexplicably great. It became obvious that in the next few months, he would emerge the richest and most prominent man in town.

"Business success brings responsibility!". His family members and relations started asking for his assistance. "What a nuisance! Was it all it means to be rich?", the man stunned in anger.

"Not you and I!", was his last comment. Following the antecedents of the story, the man left his town with all he made from his invention.

Antashi went to another town; to hide his identity, he disguised himself as a mad man. Always sitting near a dilapidated round-about all day long. Antashi caught cold which developed to acute pneumonia. He died of pneumonia.

People became interested in his story when they discovered that he had $10m on him. He was rushed to the hospital for an autopsy and it was confirmed that he died of pneumonia.

What? Die of pneumonia with $10m and as a frustrated rag-tag in an open place. There could be something else. It became breaking news... And the truth followed. It was an incredible truth!

Business success attracts responsibilities. If you fail to be responsible, it will go or you will go for it. This is an ugly story you may say, but it could be right there with you. How responsible are you with what you have?

The story in the scripture concerning the talents rightly buttresses the fact that you stand to lose what you have if you fail to use it for its purpose- Read Matt

25:14-28.

This rung of the business success ladder may be hated by many climbers, but it cannot be avoided. Giving is the flow path to opulence. It obeys both the natural law of attraction and divine principles.

God's riches acknowledge responsibility. This is a rule you must keep for your business to excel. If any business is not responsible it is not of God... Yeah!

"But how can one be responsible ?" Jeff asked. His voice portrayed he could be a victim. His question was well timed, it was my next point.

TAKING RESPONSIBILITIES

The master is the Chief servant, so is the rich. God gives wealth so that it could be used for different purposes.

Solve family problems

Problems or challenges are inevitable in families, your

business success could be a solution. Let it respond to the challenges of your: Brothers, sisters, parents...

Don't withhold your success from your neighbours, relatives and friends. As much as you can, be a solution to their challenges through your assistance .

Help the Needy

God owns and controls all things, He may not be personally interested in how much you give Him, but He is interested in the assistance you render to others (the needy). God multiplies your business when you give to the sick, the poor and the less privileged.

Kingdom Commitment

God doesn't need your gift as it were, but teaches you how to multiply your business. This is done through kingdom commitment.

God teaches success principles by asking us to invest in His Kingdom service. This is no doubt why kingdom investors are always successful. No one invests faithfully in the work of God without a genuine amazing testimony.

Think of a sorrow-free business, invest in the kingdom

of God.

The Scripture says, "Give and it will come back to y o u , good measure pressed down, shaken together and running over-shall men give unto your bosom".

Again it says, "He who sows sparingly will reap sparingly and he who sows bountifully will reap bountifully... For whatsoever a man soweth that will he reap".

Business success brings responsibilities. It is a divine mandate for you to serve humanity and God with your wealth. Don't block the channel of opulence.

These business creation lessons were re-setting the students in a perfect form to create business capable of generating opulence.

Each week with the students always deposits a new joy in me. I knew it was a sign of better things ahead. The students' performance was splendid. I had no doubt that I was working with great entrepreneurs. I had enough reason to thank God - His supplies were ever sufficient.

Thank you Lord!

Secret No. 34

The sure way of creating a lasting business is to be responsible. Invest in others and in the kingdom service.

LESSON 16

THOUGHT PATTERN AND MIND PLATFORM

This story got me thinking: A man was stoned to death by some religious fanatics due to what they called blasphemy. They said that the man made a statement which was contrary to what they were taught about their creator.

It was in a small village in West Africa. "Philosopher", the man was called due to his witty assertions which were similar to the words of great philosophers. Philosopher made his last assertion the day he said, "Man is the creator of his destiny". That was a big blasphemy they said, a fight against their religious belief and death penalty was the punishment. Philosopher was stoned to death to avenge the wrath of their god.

As I went through this story taking a closer look at Philosopher's assertion, something dropped down my mind. There was a point Philosopher wanted to portray in his assertion - the power of the mind.

Your thought pattern positions your destiny. What you

think is what you are. The scripture says, "As a man thinketh in his heart so is he" (Prov. 23:7). So you can change your thought pattern, to change what you will be. Was this not what "Philosopher" was trying to portray. Or don't you know that you can create a thought as well as destroy a thought if you want... But Philosopher has gone! Explore your imagination

See above limitations. Reason beyond odds. Think the best outcome in business. Imagine all things are possible. Be positively inclined in your thought.

Activate the image of your business destiny in your mind. Have a picture of what you desire. Define your mind-set. Be plain and specific in your pursuit. Now, build your business empire on your mind, then translate it through plan and strategies...

Think Rich

Your thought pattern matters. Think rich if you want to be rich. What you garbage into your mind is what it releases as a product.

Look at the society, those who believe that being rich is evil and ungodly get poor and poorer, whereas those who believe that being rich is a Godly heritage get rich and richer (ruminate over this). It is a practical issue.

There is no magic behind this, it only underscores the fact that your thought pattern creates your destiny. God is omniscient, He is not a dummy... His word says, "As a man thinketh in his heart so is he". He said it because He knows all things.

You are rich if you think you are rich and poor if you think you are poor. What you will be can never be different from what you think. It may delay but it must surely come to pass if you work on it.

Speak riches to your moribund business! Prophesy life and viability; and think the possibility of becoming rich (you will).

Believe You Can

Your thought provokes your believe (faith). The best way to have positive believe is to think of positive possibilities.

You are a co-heir with Jesus, a descendant of Abraham. Believe that the blessing of Abraham and the rich heritage of Jesus Christ are your portion.

Believe you can! The scripture cannot be broken it says,"I can do all things through Christ that strenghteneth me". Please appropriate this to yourself!

Business success cannot be thrown down from heaven like Manner, it is produced through your believe and the idea that comes to you. "What you believe you will achieve", says Robert Schuller.

Say What You Believe

If God was a deaf-mute the world would have still been without form and void. Contrary to this, all things were created by the word of His mouth. He said "Let there be..." And they came to be.

There is power in the word of the mouth. God has also given us the unction to function through the words of our mouth. You can close your destiny by closing your mouth , because nobody will say it for you.

Say what you believe! Be positive. God's wisdom is profitable to direct: it says,"When men say, there is a casting down, say there is a lifting up". Believe it is well with you and it shall be well. Your faith need to work, walk and talk!

Remember, no amount of negative confession can add a cubit of positive change to your destiny.

You always heard me say, "I must hit it big!" Even when there was nothing to show for it. The story will amaze you at the end. I never missed my target! With your mouth decree a blossom destiny to your business and it shall come to pass. God as already approved it when he said "Decree a thing and it shall come to pass". Say it now! Not just within your mind, but through your lips. Express yourself possitively!

Attitude Creates Business

An author said, "Your attitude determines your altitude". You can go as far as you position yourself to go. How much you are able to stretch your sling determines how far you will shoot. Does that make sense to you?

If you have a cold attitude towards business success, you can never have it. But if you crave for it as your covenant right, you must possess it. You can create business success with a positive attitude.

MIND IS THE CENTRE OF EXPLOITS

The mind is the heart of exploits. It generates the tools that creates business. The mind controls the actions of the body. Rene Desserts could not deny this fact he said, "It is the function of the mind to exercise full control over the will of the mind". Plutarch alerts us, "The mind is not a vessel to be filled but a fire to be kindled". "Great minds have purpose, little minds have wishes", says Washington Irving. Wit and Wisdom nailed these facts, "You will never be a success until you train your mind to be success conscious".

You can hit your success target by training your mind to be success conscious and use it to control your body to generate business.

Don't limit your exploits

God has never given man limits to business creation, so don't limit yourself. He has given us unlimited success. He said to Abraham, "As far as your eye can see, you will possess..." (Gen.13:14). Seeing is not limited to the physical sight but also the spirit or mind realm... Because the scope of Abraham's sight was unlimited - he had everything. We are the descendants of Abraham, by covenant his blessing and heritage are our birth right. You can be richer than Abraham because God has approved it so. "The glory of the later house shall exceed the former..." (Haggai 2:9). Don't limit your exploits, you can be a global champion, not a local champion. Explore and you shall possess. I quite agree with the words of Napoleon Hill "There is no limitation to the mind except those we acknowledge". Don't limit your mind, aim at great exploits.

Live Out Your Value

Some people create big business empire, but live wretched What a failure!

Success should be enjoyed... But not to be squandered. Live out your value. When you were studying the principles of generating wealth through business exploits at the early part of the lessons, you were placed on different restrictions because business was still far on the way. But that was far from living a wretched life. The purpose of business success is to give comfort. You are a prince, don't live like a slave. Remember, salvation includes prosperity.1 John 1:3

I discovered something about the lessons, they also showed on the reactions of the students. It was obvious that they have been looking at business creation from only one perspective- business exploits. As soon as I started combining business principles with divine principles of business creation, their attitudes changed- it created new feelings.

This is exactly what makes this book a unique book,

God has inspired it to teach you how you can combine divine wisdom with business principles to create success.

The divine aspect was a big lacuna in the students business plan (little wonder they couldn't escape failure).

If you have followed the lessons diligently, as you climb the last rung of the business creation ladder to behold "God as the owner"; your business, career, marriage and all your undertakings shall never see failure in Jesus name, Amen!

This is the only prophetic prayer in this book... God has liberated you from your ugly past to place you on a pleasant destiny.

Secret No. 35

Your positive thinking takes you to the place of your business creation. Let your thought be unlimited.

Authors 'Views

The views of these great author formed the crux of lesson sixteen. After a critical analysis of over five hundred world's richest men, Napoleon Hill wrote his book, "Think and grow rich". That was because he came to the knowledge that all riches are products of positive thinking. He asserted, "Both poverty and riches are the offspring of thought". This finding must have to motivated Robert Kiyosaki when he mused, "If you want more money change your thinking." Think rich!

LESSON 17

MAXIMIZE YOUR IDEA

You have just entered a unique level of realizing your dream. Get ready to create and reposition your business.

This is the great business success secret... I had an unusual joy because we were on the hotspot.

Hear it again, your idea is supreme. This lesson unveils the secret power of the greatest business concept. You must maximize your idea for the best outcome in business creation.

THE KING RESOURCE

Idea is the impulse which drops down your mind and seek to inform, suggest, direct or build a new reality within you.

It is like a mustard seed; very small in size, yet could turn to a giant tree. It is gentle and noiseless in nature and could come like a drop depositing an eternal resource in the mind which could built a business empire.

Idea is the raw material, the thriving platform of business success. It is a malleable resource that can be readily converted to wealth and make ones dreams and aspirations real.

HOW IDEA COMES

Idea is the product of thought, it sizzles from the inner mind and boldly comes out the door of our thought. Some ideas drop quietly in a still moment, others strike the mind when there is stress, pressure or necessity. How it comes doesn't matter, yet we should be absolutely diligent how we handle this special guest.

The concept of idea in this book is specifically narrowed to godly and resourceful idea. Having the cognizance that there could be evil or ungodly ideas, we should understand that only godly idea brings good success.

HOW IDEA GENERATES SUCCESS

"Nobody has money problem, only an idea problem",

says Robert Schuller. You must have wasted the whole of your life time trying to find the solution to your financial problem without success. Yes, you can't fix it because you don't have financial problem. What you have is idea problem. Idea takes one beyond solving a financial problem, but is capable of solving all problems to give one a distinctive position an unbeatable business success.

Believe in your idea, it is not inferior as you think. It is unique and of global standard. You are swallowed by low self-esteem - the fear that your idea will be rejected by professionals, but what you failed to know is that you can equally be a professional. Professionals are mere amateurs who persisted in their ideas. You too can be a professional.

You can be a first class in your field if you can recognize, nurse, nurture, develop and sell your idea

.Why not turn your ideas into assets and use them to generate a lifetime success magnate.

THE RATTLING QUESTION

Kellen asked, "Why is it that some people succeed at almost everything they venture while some never succeeded in anything?". I gazed at him with a smile and thought for the right answer. Not before I could answer his question, he remarked, "I never succeeded in anything I do, why?" His face was ashen and his countenance completely impassive.

I first worked on his countenance before I listed some success nuggets that would help him overcome his problem. I explained them vividly, but he seemed to be very close to these success nuggets. Oh yes! I looked at him again- this time more carefully and asked, " How do you maximize your idea?". He lifted his face and asked, "What idea?" "The ideas that come to your mind", I replied. His eyes dilated with anxiety, "Oh, different ideas come to my mind, but I don't like working on them, they could be stressful", he said.

Yes, I realized why he hadn't succeeded. I took time to explain to him how his ideas could make the difference. "Try this secret power of success, it must fetch you a fortune", I assured him.

Before we parted, I removed a sheet of paper and wrote some steps to guide him achieve success through the idea that comes to his mind.

THE GUIDELINE

If you discard resourceful ideas that come to your mind just like Kellen, now is the right time to correct your mistakes by building on your ideas. Explore this mastermind hotspot.

Recognize An Idea

The first step is to recognize an idea. Take time to think, an idea comes to your mind like an impulse. Treat it like a special guest, and don't be in a haste to discard it. Remember that an idea is an offspring of thought, a picture of your potential (it represents who you are).

Hold those thoughts that come to your mind constantly - it is natural. Never think of mastering somebody's idea, but recognize those ideas that come to your mind- they are the platform to your greatness.

Don't force yourself to sing when you have nothing to show for it, rather look for what you have - it makes you special, different and fulfilled.

God deposited in every one sufficient resources to make one succeed - they are the ideas that come to your mind.

Pause here and ruminate for a while... Can you recall a thought that constantly rock your mind? Yes, it is resourceful and comes from time to time... Yeah, the one you always neglected. Can you recollect?

Great men we hear about today were ordinary men who recognized the resourceful ideas that came to them and were able to utilize the ideas to mount on the success ladder.

Listen to this, if no idea is on your mind, start from "What can I do?" to "How can I do it?" Think of a big challenge; look for a solution... Something must strike your mind right now!

Write It Down

Now, pick up your pen, it is another important step. You can do your self a favour if you can listen to yourself. Don't let anything distract you. Think! If you can still remember an idea that constantly strike your mind, write it down. This will help you to always remember it.

Author John Benson wrote, "Nothing dies so quickly than an idea in a closed mind". What an inspiration!

Now that you have written it down, look at it the second time. Do you have any comment to make? What? Unique, natural - that's the picture of yourself (your potentials).

Be Original in Your Idea

You may never perfect in somebody's idea, you can perfect in your own idea. Never think of copying or imitating somebody's idea, it is a waste and a mark of failure.

Idea is the picture of potentials; a unique and natural resource, the fountain of your success. Be careful, don't let people's opinion or what they do affect the product of your idea. Be original and work with maximum concentration. Your original idea will distinguish you and give you the desired success.

Nurse and Nurture Your Idea

Slow your pace, don't be in a hurry. This exercise is a bit psychological, you need to know this...

Now that you can see your idea in black and white, expand your mind to absorb it. Ensure that you create room for improvement. Don't let this special guest to be crushed by negativism or environmental factors.

Protect your idea like a mother would unto a young child. Look at it as a "saviour" capable of pulling you out of the shackles of failure. It is honourable, please address it so.

Reshape and Develop Your Idea

An idea may be very small in size - just like a dot. You still have a work to do. There could be need to reshape an idea. You can do this by going to the future (your target) in the realm of your mind looking also at the idea before you. Your ultimate aim is to succeed, you are tied of being a failure.

You can reshape the idea before you to meet your target. This may involve additions and subtractions, all to ensure you meet your expected desire.

Develop an idea to focus on the areas of need, consider market first. Shape your idea to be focused and develop it to be large and productive.

Something is about to happen! You are on the verge of attracting the attention of the world. Congratulations!

Never say, "What if I fail?". That's not the language of people who want to succeed. You try again. Alright!

Carefully look at your developed idea again to know whether there are still few things to add or subtract. Can you find one? Remember, your idea is unique and you are about to blaze a trail.

You can now take a recess. Your brain seems to need a little rest. Pause here before you take the next step!

Test Your Idea

Welcome back! Hope you enjoyed the short break. We have finally entered the nitty-gritty of your effort to succeed through your idea. No doubt you would like to know how you fared.

Your name will soon be written in the world's success hall of fame. What an honour! No no, don't be nervous! There is no need to panic...

You have finally distinguished yourself. You will be celebrated for your outstanding success. What a privilege!

Idea reveals the pathway through which success come back to you. Remember that your ultimate focal point is to succeed; to make this possible, there must be returns from the product of your idea. Test if the product of your idea is sellable. Can it be exchanged for a reward? This concept is termed "Market Demand Analysis". If your test is positive, stand bold to announce your success. Say to yourself, "I am rich!".

Bravo! You are about to enjoy a new world - the world of success. Bye to failure and stagnation. God has helped you to discover this amazing secret power. Don't hide it, let other people know about this secret of success. They equally need it as much as you do.

Advertize Your Idea

There is no doubt you are happy that your idea tested positive. Your status has automatically changed, but you still have a work to do. Remember that the degree of your success depends on this step you are about to take. Here, you are giving the opportunity to determine how successful you want to be. How successful do I want to be? Let this question be on your mind as you step out to actualize your ambition.

Open your mind! It won't be enough for you to settle as a mediocre - being satisfied with average. Shoot your advert to fetch you the huge success you desire.

The society has taken a new phase... Changes that follow development is on the increase; you must let people know where you are and what you have before they will recognize and celebrate you. Let the society know about your idea - advertize it!

When you crave the indulgence of people concerning what you have (the product of your idea), it will sell you. Don't be shy to let people know what you have. Be proud to announce your ability - that's the sure way to achieving success.

Sell Your Idea

Now that you have craved the indulgence of the society about your idea, let me also congratulate you again.

Do well to identify a suitable market for your idea. Let me remind you that your idea has now been converted to a marketable commodity with effective demand.

Find a place to sell this commodity. Remember that when you were developing your idea, you considered areas of need. Alright! Please locate these areas of need now. Have you done that? It is the place the product of your idea (your new commodity) is needed.

If the commodity is service oriented, please do it with diligence and honesty. And if it is goods, give the best quality. Never produce substandard products or render half-baked service.

The quality of your commodity depends on the quality of your idea, be diligent when you work on your idea. Let the products of your idea create market for itself... Let it sell you!

To my surprise the guideline took more sheets of paper than I expected. Kenneth sat quietly staring at me as I wrote. It was a wonderful evening.

As a footnote, I summarized all the vital points I explained in the guidelines thus: Secret powers of idea and numbered them one to twenty-seven for easy reference.

SECRET POWERS OF IDEA

1. Ideas are technologies for business success creation.

2. Ideas represent who you are.

3. Ideas are pictures of potentials and abilities.

4. You will remain where you are unless you catch the ideas that come to you.

5. The thing that happens in your environment is not as important as the one that happens inside of you - your idea.

6. Your idea is natural with you.

7. Idea reveals uniqueness and creativity.

8. You can't perfect in somebody's idea, you can perfect in your own idea.

9. Take time to think, idea comes to your mind like an impulse.

10. Lay hold on those ideas that come to your mind constantly.

11. Be natural, believe in your ideas.

12. Don't try t o master somebody's idea, it is a waste and pathway to failure.

13. Start from "What can I do?" to "How can I do it?"

That's how ideas come and success achieved.

14. Idea looks for areas of need.

15. You are in the position of the quality of your idea.

16. Idea reveals a pathway through which success come back to you.

17. Your idea will sell you!

18. Create for yourself a market to sell your idea and develop a strategy to sell it.

19. Ideas are indispensable source o f success.

20. To develop an idea, ask right questions and find right answers to them.

21. Know the right time and the appropriate place to sell your idea.

22. Idea leads to creativity and creativity leads to success.

23. Idea is the product of thought.

24. Idea is the heart, the engine of civilization without it mankind would still be living in caves.

25. Professionals are mere armatures who persisted in their ideas.

26. Success doesn't mean making it fast, but it is a

sustained progress without

obstructing the progress of others.

27. Every invention in this world originated from somebody's idea.

THE BOLD CONFESSION

One Saturday morning, Kellen visited. His visit was a big surprise. He hadn't visited at that hour of the day. 6:00am was such an early hour to expect him; something must be wrong, my mind flip flopped.

They were also two, I thought there could be a problem. No, their countenance contradicted my worries. Yet, I was impatient to allow them say what they came for.

"What's the matter?", I asked. "It worked!", Kellen thundered almost jumping up. "What do you mean?", I asked again trying to understand him well. "Of course, the secret power", Kellen announced with a bold smile. Kellen raised his head, he was now more serious. "Where have you been, so you have not listened to the advert?". His tone was more of a surprise than a question.

"Advert ?", I retorted, getting more confused. He looked at Joe and both laughed. Their laugh was loud and noisy with a pitch almost unbearable. It lasted about two minutes and few seconds. I watched them as they laughed. I knew they were saying something important, I only needed more explanation to understand the little puzzle.

"Alright!", Kellen said; "I am glad to tell you that the secret power has made me a hero, I now run the hottest business in town. I have joined the list of the world's inventors".

I listened with undistorted enthusiasm as he narrated the experience of his new world in some what amazing way. "That's wonderful, congratulations!", I appreciated his exploits.

There is no doubt that you will like to know what he invented. I shall tell you, but I also want you to invent something with the empowerment and the knowledge of the secret power that generates success you have acquired in this chapter; you should also tel others about your invention. Did you say -yes? If you make it a promise, you can now read Kellen's invention below.

KELLEN'S INNOVATION

Kellen was able to write down an idea which constantly struck his mind. He nursed, nurtured, developed and tested it. His thought about the possibility of producing a mechanism capable of controlling house-hold appliances which were manually operated gave birth a remote device to control curtains, doors, windows and regulate fans by a mere click on the buttons of the remote device

It took Kellen few weeks to develop his idea. He engaged in a research which helped him to gather different elements which could carry out his proposed task and mechanisms to be attached to the curtains, doors, windows and fans to perfectly respond to the inbuilt applications in the remote control device.

Yes, it worked! Kellen invented a remote device capable of controlling curtains, doors, windows, and regulating fans just by a mere click on the buttons of the remote machine.

It was advertized on radio and television stations. Many wanted to know how it worked. The demand was high and returns unspeakably great.

That's splendid! Somebody has climbed the ladder of

success. You too can do it. It's all about purpose, plan and determination. Think! Create! Idea is supreme.

Please go back to the guidelines and follow the steps diligently. You have no reason to die a failure when you have an idea capable of making you a hero.

I can see the fear of failure, negativism and low self esteem still holding you back. Rise to this challenge, you too can succeed.

When Kellen finished narrating his exploits, Joe turned to me, looking a bit distressed, he asked in somewhat timid tone, "Will this secret power always work? What will be the next action when it fails to work?".

Listen, one who wants to succeed doesn't ask this type of question. This question is a typical mind set of one controlled by fear of failure and negativism. In case you are like Joe, you want to know if the amazing technology that generates success works always.

The simple answer is "yes!". There is no need to panic. It is a sure -bet to success - let faith guide you... There is no failure anywhere until you quit trying. Patience is virtue.

It will be interesting to talk about some of the world's successful men who applied this secret power and climbed the ladder of success.

MANIFESTATIONS OF IDEA

We have discovered that idea is the secret power that generates success. But before we seal our conclusion, let me bring to our minds some successful men in the annals of history of the world, who utilized their ideas and invented machines which pushed the world to its present level of development.

Due to the exploits of these men, it should therefore be rightly stated that idea is the heart, the engine of civilization without it mankind would still be living in caves.

CHARLES BARBAGE: In 1944, his idea resulted to a computer which turned the world into a "global village".

BILL GATES: In 2006, his name ran top in the world's success hall of fame when he invented the Microsoft in computer software. He was named the world's richest man.

JOHANN GUTENBERG: A German who invented printing press in 1456

ZACHARIA JARSEEN: A Dutchman who invented "Compound Microscope in 1590.

GALIEO GALILEI: He was Italian who invented Telescope in 1609.

JAMES WATT: James Watt, a Scottish who invented the first Steam Engine in 1663.

COMTEDE SIVARAC: A Frenchman who invented Bicycle in 1790

MICHAEL FARADAY: Michael Faraday, an Englishman who invented electricity in 1913.

THIMONIER: A Frenchman, he invented Sewing Machine in 1830.

WILLIAM FOX TAIBOT: An Englishman, he invented Camera in 1835.

GLIDDEN SHOLES: An American, he invented Typewriter in 1867.

CART BENE: A German, he invented the first Motor Car in 1885.

W. K RONTGEN

W.K. Rontgen was a German who invented X - rays.

CRVILLET AND WIBUR WRIGHT: Two Americans who invented Airplane in 1903.

To crown the World access to communication, the Global System Mobile (GSM) was an idea of European which started in 1982 when the European Post and Telegraphs (EPT) formed a study group called Group Special Mobile (GSM).

This was however handed over to another group in 1989 - The European Telecommunication Standard Institute (ETSI) called Group Special Mobile (GSM).

In 1990, the government of United Kingdom (UK) requested the specification for GSM based on a high upper densities with low power mobile stations operating at 1.9 GHZ. Within the space of five years, the GSM became operational in over 60 countries with over 5.4 million subscribers.

The list of World inventors could go endless. Inventions are product of ideas and ideas of thoughts. Ideas are unique and natural. The best way to start is to get started. You can develop your ideas and ride on your business success.

LESSON 18

THE WILLPOWER STRATEGY

The Eighteenth rung of the ladder of business creation exposes the eighteenth lesson which marks the eighteenth week of the inception of the noble dream of climbing a business ladder. It's last rungs will give you access to the creative idea for your business empire. This is a purposeful journey of twenty-one weeks...

You may never have embarked on this type of journey before - a journey with strenuous training. Patience is the virtue to keep you. It is late to be a mediocre - don't back out! You are almost there, what you need is more determination. You can be impacted with relevant ideas for business creation.

The eighteenth lesson is the concluding lesson of the third academic session in the Business Creation School. I am proud of all the students (including you)

The willing heart creates business

The heart is the starting point of all business creation. The willingness of the mind to create business generates desire and enthusiasm to achieve it.

John Heywood rightly observed this fact when he said, "Nothing is impossible to a willing heart" Little wonder, the Scripture speaks in the same vein, "If you are willing and obedient thou shall eat the good of the land" (Isaiah 1:19).

This means you can create and possess treasures of the land just by switching on your will. The will is the fountain of thirst, hunger, quest and desire which generates zeal/enthusiasm for positive result. Willpower = thirst /hunger - quest /desire-zeal/enthusiasm - work/ask = business success.

This dual-chain chat flow generate business success through the willpower.

This secret could have motivated the preaching of David Ambrose he said, "If you have the will to win you have achieved half your success, if you don't, you have achieved half your failure".

There is no way without the will

"But without thy mind would I do nothing; that thy benefit should not be as it were of necessity but of willingness", Philemon:14

One cannot get to his destination in the dark without a light, nor can the body claim to master everything without the eyes.

The will is the light that shows the direction to the destination. The will is the spirit energy which says "Let there be...". How the earth would have remained void if the spirit of God did not hover the surface of the earth and empower (activate) the word as God said, "Let there be... " And they came into being.

There is no way without the will -business can't be generated if the spirit energy (will) is dormant. All things are possible, if there is a will!

Use Your Will To Create Your Business

It is as simple as it sounds. Now that you have a business plan, activate your will. This is the life that makes your business function. The will is the spirit man in your business. Let your will generate strong determination to arrive at your success quest destination.

Keep moving, you must draw from the well of riches!

Secret No. 37

Your willpower lightens your way to create business. Have the will to create business, it must answer you.

LESSON 19

TAKE STOCK AND GROW YOUR CONFIDENCE

The new academic session started with a smooth sail. It is always a great joy seeing ones destination in view. We must hit it big!

Matt, Jeff, Nic, Dan, Chizo, Jessy... And "You", have all been wonderful students.

Remember, this school wouldn't be complete if you had not enrolled (by reading this book). You made a wise decision to stir up your creative power. It takes only one purposeful and hardworking person to become great. All you need to complete your business empire is to stay glued to the remaining lessons. Connect to the mastermind...

Looking down the ladder from nineteenth rung, the distance covered was much. It is only those who are bond to fail that would think of giving up this noble task - but not you!

I knew it was pertinent for appraisal to reflect on who

or what one was and the new status on the ladder of business creation.

Take stock!

Stock taking is a form of appraisal. It is very important in business management practice.

There should be a time for self or business assessment to know what you have or lack. You are on your way to discover opulence - the way up is guided by principles and secrets to ensure harmony.

Think like these:

* Have I understood the secrets of business creation?

* Can I apply the principles?

* What new things have I learnt that are different from what I knew or think?

* Have I been able to adjust to the new knowledge?

* What would be the best strategy for me to hit my target?

* There are two parts to realizing my vision - the business part and the Divine part. How well have I understood each part? Can I combine them to

produce a desired result?

Why take stock?

This is an important exercise to :

* Access yourself and your business

* To improve on your efforts where necessary.

* To correct your errors /lags and lacks.

* To prepare yourself to advance to your target.

I allowed the students some minutes of self-appraisal to discover their new position.

Do you think you can create business with your idea? Nic was the first to answer, but all answered, "Yes!". What do you say?

The real you

The real "you" is what you need to discover. It positions you towards your exploits. The real "you" is in you. This is why your destiny lies on your choice. What do you think concerning your potentials and the creative knowledge you have acquired? There is a work to do! How much you are able to enable your ability brings out the "real you" in you. Exercise your idea.

Pastor Edwin Ogelenya reminds us, "What will make you meaningful in life is already in you". This is the real you. But you don't stop at discovering the real you - go on to explore it. Innocent Ngwee advises, "Energies are not to be stored, but to be used to generate success". Yes, create your business empire.

This is why you need not relent until you hit your target. The real you makes you who you are. Sydney Harris rightly observed, "Ninety percent of the world's woes come from people not knowing themselves, their abilities, their frailties and even their real virtues".

Think! Can you see the real you? Your idea?

* It is not in the fear, it is in the faith.

* It is not in the failure, it is in the forward.

* It is not in the impossibility, but in the all possibility.

* It is not in the past, it is in the present and future.

* It is not in others, it is in you.

* It is not in the negative attitude, but in the positive attitude .

* It is not who you thought you were , it is who you

just discovered you are .

* It is capable of creating the business you desire.

Take stock. See the real you! Keep on the onward track until you build your business empire.

"The higher you go, the cooler it becomes" was a scientific assertion I learnt during my early school years. This assertion is wide in scope, I discovered later. It is also true in business creation (business science if you like).

Quite amazing! The rungs were becoming easier to climb and the initial confusion which had always shown in the students questions have gone down.

The enthusiasm is maximum, but the stress and confusion minimum. This made me to agree with Daniel Webster when he said, "There is always room at the top". You will yet discover this truth when you climb the last rung.

Secret No. 40

Always take stock of yourself and business, it will help you to improve. You will find the real you! Your idea is supreme.

LESSON 20

CREATE BUSINESS SUCCESS PILLARS

The twentieth rung exposes the pillars of business creation. The strength of any structure most times lies on the strength of the supporting pillars. Even when the foundation is strong, the pillars still play their role for the structure to stand and last.

You can create business and enjoy opulence when you lean on the success pillars.

Remember, how fast a structure is built doesn't count, but how long it lasts. Use these pillars to support your business structure.

KNOWLEDGE

Business is never created in ignorance. Knowledge is the light which dismisses ignorance to create business.

Ignorance brings fear but knowledge brings faith. Faith creates business. Knowledge gives you access to the secrets and principles of business creation. It exposes and teaches you the mechanism which business is generated.

What you know determines what you will be. God says in the Scripture, "My people perish because of lack of knowledge", Hosea 4:6.

Some people never got it right because they are not informed. When you are not informed, you are deformed. Information gives knowledge. An author rightly observed that the difference between the rich and the poor is information (yes, knowledge).

What you know distinguishes you from the crowd. That is why this book was inspired to give you a new knowledge capable of creating your business.

* Knowledge teaches

* Knowledge informs

* Knowledge enlightens

* Knowledge creates faith.

* Knowledge exposes ignorance and establishes confidence.

The knowledge of business principles are combined with divine Principles to create lasting business is what positions you better than your contemporaries.

Knowledge is simply the deposit of "know-how" - a way of doing something. Business creation responds to knowledge. It is what you know that you go on to create. Knowledge create business, don't ignore it!

UNDERSTANDING

Understanding opens your intellectual power to assimilate. This comes through meditation on the words of knowledge. Through understanding, the secrets and principles of business creation are interpreted.

Understanding is the insight that perfects knowledge. Build your wealth with understanding but not without knowledge.

WISDOM

Wisdom is the applied part of the knowledge for wealth creation. It puts the secrets and principles of wealth creation to work.

Business success is always associated with wisdom,

"The wisdom of God is the commander of success", says Bishop David Oyedepo. He further asserted, "Wisdom and success are intertwined such that wherever you find true wisdom, success accompanies it."

This exposes to us the secret of king Solomon's wealth. God gave him wisdom and wealth followed it. Business is created by wisdom. This means that you cannot fail in business with the wisdom of God. Hence, you can only create a business empire like king Solomon through the wisdom of God.

THE THREE PILLARS

Knowledge, understanding and wisdom may be difficult to be separated (they are three in one). Business creation responds to the combination of these three.

The trio could be hard to be separated because they are interrelated. "Happy is the man who finds wisdom and the man who gets understanding, for the gain from it is better than gold… Long life is in her right hand, in her left hand are riches and honour" (Proverb 3: 13-14 and 16).

"Does not wisdom call, does not understanding raise

her voice?" (Proverbs 8:1)"They are straight to him who find knowledge" (Prov, 8: 9.)

The knowledge, understanding and wisdom of the divine secrets and principles of business creation empower the knowledge, understanding and wisdom of business secrets and principles to generate success.

The Divine Factor

The importance of the divine factor in business creation could be highlighted thus:

* It makes business creation possible without tears or sorrow.

* Business can always be created and can always crumble. It is the divine factor that guarantees business success.

* To live in peace and enjoy wealth; "It is only the blessings of God that make rich an addeth no sorrow".

* To acknowledge God as the owner, giver and creator of wealth (Duet. 8:18)

Any business created no matter how strong can collapse if it is not of God. Therefore, it takes God to sustain business success.

"For the Lord gives wisdom; from his mouth come knowledge and understanding", (Proverbs 2: 6.).

God is the source of the pillars of business creation. He gives these pillars through His words. Remember, faith creates business. "And faith comes by hearing, and hearing the word of God", (Romans 10:17.)

Secret No. 40

Knowledge, understanding and wisdom of God are the three pillars of business creation.

The Bottom Line

Trust in the Lord with all your might and lean not in your own understanding. In all your ways acknowledge Him and He will give you the pillars of business creation (paraphrased).

I concluded lesson twenty by telling the students that the pillars could be acquired by searching and discovering the secrets and principles of business creation in the word of God.

LESSON 21

YOUR BALANCE SHEET SHOWS YOUR WINNING HABITS

I must hit it big! I always professed. My sub-conscious mind has received and accepted this fact and it has started reflecting on me (physically).

This lesson started in a high spirit. Yes, the boat is on the habour. The hand-bills and posters were all over town. They announced the vision in a unique dimension. The Newspaper, radio and television also advertised it.

Enrollment would commence a week before formal resumption. The adverts carried every detail of the business creation school.

The support was terrific. Money is now in business, ready to play its inevitable role to complement the mastermind...

Lives have been transformed to create business. It was a sweet morning of great testimonies. Matt, Jeff and Nic all had their turns to express their joy and experiences. Somebody is already on the path of business success!

THE BALANCE SHEET

The balance sheet reveals the state and size of your efforts. It shows where your are. Business is all about profitability. The amount of profit is indicated by the size of the balance sheet. Let your balance sheet go beyond financial increase, general welfare is important.

Create business through your value oriented idea. Let your idea be a solution or an answer to a big question. Think and be who you want be:

* A celebrity

* A success

* A merchant

* An entrepreneur

Don't be limited, think of being the best. Be the best in your choice career. Create your relevance.

Look up... It's up to you! I hope you are ready to launch into a new horizon. Business success is sure!

What a good coincidence; the graduation day was also

my birth date in the second month of the year.

That morning, I had just gone to supervise the new site of the business creation school. What I saw was inexplicably amazing. The work was perfect. I had no doubt that the dream has turned a reality.

Immediately, I started planning for the formal inauguration of Lun Sage Business School - I thought of publicity, staff recruitment and payment; code of conduct, etc. More and more my plan expanded.

I sat back to have an overview of my work, a thought flashed - "The Vision". I paused to think for an appropriate one: Light unto nations in character, learning and creativity.

Exploring the 4Ps of marketing mix

I allowed different marketing promotional strategies to play: the print media, radio, television and social media. All conveyed the desired information, creating a thriving platform for a successful business school. I went ahead to harmonize the different batches to a uniform teaching calender, where elaborate curriculum stirs the lessons with kind emphasis on the use of Career Pro Books as teaching manual.

I remembered that I had informed the students the

previous week they would review their business plans after the last lesson before they invest their money to their businesses. But I must also remind them; and I did. The lesson started in a smooth sail...

How amazing the power of imagination. The mind power creates all things. This school is in deed a product of the mind power. Thinking out my idea to reality.

Look up. It's up to you!

* Take responsibility of your business success

* You must be focused.

* What you ask for is what you get.

* If you want it big, plan it big.

* Think out what you want.

* Kill the mediocre spirit.

* Business success is within, discover it.

* You must create value first.

"I can tell how you can get what you want; you just got to keep a thing in view and go for it and never let your eyes wander to the right or left, or up or down. And looking back is fatal." A parcel of wisdom from William Lock. Author James Allen mused, "You will become as small as your controlling desire; as great as your dominant aspiration". Frank Tyger hits it further, "Your future depends on many things but mostly on you."

It Is Your Choice

Success and failure respond to choice. Each can be created or destroyed. I quite agree with Herbert Porchnow when he said, "There is a time when we must firmly choose the course which we will follow or the relentless drift of event will make the decision for us". Our choice places us on our possession. Don't choose to be a pauper or a mediocre when God has promised to honour you with his abundant treasures. You may not know, it is in your hands to make or destroy your destiny. You have the power to create!

Start somewhere, but don't stop!

There are two things to be created: success or failure. Your choice places you on either side. What are you creating? Use this book as your manual for wealth creation. Be an unlimited creator!

"There is no future in the past", an author asserted. Wealth creation ignores yesterday, but uses today to create tomorrow. Don't limit yourself - go for the best. Somerset Maughan got it right, "If you are satisfied with the good, you will never get what is best".

Right Habits Make Good Balance

* It is not what people say, it is what you say.

* It is not what people think, but what you think.

* It is not what they see, but what you see.

* You can only be limited by yourself.

* It is the will of God for you to succeed - work it out.

* Recognize the grace and mercy of God.

* You can if you think you can. Stretch your creative power.

Now, start that business with your idea. Create value first. Be bold to take a step... Your idea is supreme!

OTHER PURPOSE DRIVEN BOOKS BY THE SAME AUTHOR

(a) The Success Within

(b) Acts of Great Men

NOVELS

(a) The Dark Orbit

(b) Crested Symbol

CONTACT THE AUTHOR:

(1) Whatsapp: +2348032278159 (2) Mobile: +2348026711727

(3) Instagram: lunsage.24 (4) Facebook: Lun Sage

(5) Email: lunsage123@gmail.com

Or lazino_u@yahoo.com

ABOUT THE AUTHOR

Lun Sage is an Economist. He started his career as a banker and has worked as a

sales staff in a commercial bank for seven years before he moved to the Insurance

industry as a Senior Financial Planner and later to a leading Credit Rating / Risk

Management Agency where he led debt recovery/reconciliation team. He is a serial entrepreneur and business consultant committed to strategic business initiatives and innovations.

Lun is a certified member of NIM (Chartered) and OSHA Academy (USA). His academic background, job training and life experience are rich insights to his explicit approach in expressing his ideas... He is a renowned business coach and prolific writer.

His books: The Success Within, Acts of Great Men and The Business Secret Power are all-time goal and purpose driven books.

Lun is the CEO of CareerPro International: a publishing, marketing, mental empowerment and human resource management consult, committed to creating veritable impact to life, career and the society.

www.ingramcontent.com/pod-product-compliance
Lightning Source LLC
Chambersburg PA
CBHW021814170526
45157CB00007B/2581